GREEK REVIVAL
from the Garden

YOUNG PALMETTO BOOKS
Kim Shealy Jeffcoat, Series Editor

GREEK REVIVAL

from the Garden

Growing and Cooking for Life

Patricia Moore-Pastides

Charlie Ryan, Horticulturist

Keith McGraw, Photographer

The University of South Carolina Press

Published by the University of South Carolina Press
Columbia, South Carolina 29208

www.sc.edu/uscpress

Manufactured in China

21 20 19 18 17 16 15 14 10 9 8 7 6 5 4 3 2

Library of Congress Cataloging-in-Publication Data

Moore-Pastides, Patricia.
Greek revival from the garden : growing and cooking for life / Patricia Moore-Pastides ; Charlie Ryan, horticulturist ; Keith McGraw, photographer.
pages cm.— (Young palmetto books)
Includes bibliographical references and index.
ISBN 978-1-61117-190-7 (hardback)—ISBN 978-1-61117-191-4 (epub) (print) 1. Cooking, Mediterranean. I. Ryan, Charlie. II. McGraw, Keith. III. Title.
TX725.M35M66 2013
641.59182'2—DC23 2012043713

Frontispiece: Bitter melon on our garden gate

For Jean Coleman Moore and Penelope Jean Erickson

Peas

Contents

Carrots

Preface

You've probably heard by now that we Americans are the fattest people ever to have walked the earth, and as a result we're getting more and more unhealthy.

Is the problem with our food supply? Are we just eating too many calorie-intense fast-food meals? Or is the problem with our lack of exercise? Are we sitting around watching too much television, playing too much Xbox and PlayStation, and tweeting too much about it all?

I think it's all the above, so I've written *Greek Revival from the Garden: Growing and Cooking for Life.* This book provides everything you need to cook really delicious and healthful meals for your family and friends, and it will even help you start your own garden of fresh organic fruits and vegetables regardless of whether you have a big backyard or just a sunny porch.

There is a way of eating that scientists have been studying for more than fifty years. It's called the Traditional Mediterranean Diet; let's call it TMD. Research has shown that by eating lots of fresh fruits and vegetables, whole grains, beans, nuts, seafood, and dairy in moderation, people live longer, healthier lives—often well into their nineties! The TMD doesn't include processed foods, foods that have colors or chemicals added, or foods heavy with animal fats and sodium like typical American fast foods.

The best news about the TMD is that, even if you don't grow your own, the ingredients are easy to find. The cooking methods are simple. And the tastes are really delicious!

Greek Revival from the Garden: Growing and Cooking for Life brings you two terrific skills that you'll use your whole life—growing your own food and cooking it in the TMD way.

Warning 1: If you really get into the TMD, you may find that you can't eat fast food anymore because it tastes too salty and leaves your teeth feeling greasy!
Warning 2: If you really get into the TMD, you may end up cooking for your family and friends. Not everybody is willing to try something new at first, but once they try it, well—be prepared for a landslide of compliments!

I had a secret reason for writing this book: gardening and cooking are by far and away the best chores around the house! If I had known how to raise vegetables and cook when I was younger, I could have avoided cleaning out the linen closet!

Happy gardening and cooking!

A NOTE ON THE DEDICATION

One of the most wonderful aspects of gardening is being in the natural world, becoming more deeply aware, more sensitive to the cycle of life: germination, growth, blossoming, fruiting, seeding, and even dying as the soil is ultimately replenished by decomposing plant materials. Before gardening I never thought about the dying season of plants, but I felt it. In New England I sensed a time of sadness after the glorious red, orange, and gold foliage when the earth was overcast in brown and the sky grayed.

Still I didn't expect to be so energized by a move to the South. But the ever-present sunshine invigorated my body and spirit as I'd wake up each day to the newfound energy of the sun.

As I write this, it's actually raining: good, I don't have to fight with myself to stay focused at my desk, and I'm reminded of how seriously we need this rain. Another life force of the natural world, rain perks up even the tail end of the scraggly cucumber vines and the toppling brown-edged tomato bushes.

I have dedicated this book to two very special people. The first is well-known to me: my beautiful mother, Jean Coleman Moore. Over the years I've teased her about avoiding doctors, but in many ways she has followed her own path to healthy aging. She lives very naturally and is a healthy eater. Her diet is mainly vegetables, but she does eat some meats and fish at times. She doesn't smoke or drink (except when we celebrated her seventy-fifth birthday in Ireland and I convinced her to have a "baby" Guinness).

We recently spent a week in Connecticut. When I dropped Mom off at her home after dinner one evening, I looked into her eyes: at eighty-two years of age, she looked more beautiful than ever.

I think I know why: we had spent the evening holding a precious baby girl, her skin softer than a ball of cotton, her smile so broadly stretched that it revealed a dimple just beneath her right eye, and her laugh hearty and contagious for such a tiny person.

Penelope Jean Erickson was born on April 29, 2012, and on the night I've described, she was three and a half months old but had the focused attention of a much older child. Of course I think she is a genius! She arrived in the world in time for my mother and me to be promoted on Mother's Day: Mom to "Great-Grammy" and me to "Grammy."

So I am dedicating *Greek Revival from the Garden: Growing and Cooking for Life* to these two special people in my family. Mom, my wish for you is healthy longevity that we might share our grandbaby's life for years to come and teach her to garden and to cook.

Penelope, my wish for you is that you are always surrounded by love, that you explore and have adventures that never end, and that you live every day with your special focused attention as you discover the wonders of this beautiful world. May you never smoke, always play and exercise, eat well from your garden, and take time to enjoy with all your senses this wonderful life.

Young grapes

Acknowledgments

In embarking on a book that would appeal to young adults, I was encouraged by the University of South Carolina School of Library and Information Science, specifically Kim Shealy Jeffcoat, executive director of the South Carolina Center for Children's Books and Literacy, and Helen Fellers, its coordinator and "Reading Rooster." They were first to express excitement about the project and facilitated my research.

I would not have had the confidence to write about gardening, a relatively recent avocation, without the counsel of Charlie Ryan, chief horticulturist at the University of South Carolina President's House. Charlie is knowledgeable, patient with novices, and generous in sharing his expertise. In the past year he has assisted students and staff in cultivating raised beds so they can grow their own vegetables on campus, earning the 2012 Outstanding Faculty or Staff Volunteer Award. He exemplifies the "No Limits" spirit of the University of South Carolina.

Ginger Adams and Britney Ellisor work with Charlie to keep the President's House gardens, the Historic Horseshoe, and the Russell House botanicals beautiful. And they slip in some herbs and veggies to keep things interesting! Thank you to Amanda McNulty, Tony Melton, and Cory Tanner, Clemson extension agents—and my dear friend Marcia Montgomery—for your editing and advice.

This is the second book that Keith McGraw and I have worked on together. Keith is a great photographer, who is beginning to appreciate the ease of food photography—as the dishes can't blink or start talking when he snaps. He survives long photo shoots by being the taste tester too! I value his talent and his taste buds.

I thank former Columbia's Cooking! director Katherine Shavo and University of South Carolina Cancer Prevention and Control Program (CPCP) principal investigator James Hébert for assistance in editing. The mission of Columbia's Cooking!, which is a significant activity of CPCP, is to encourage folks to cook and eat in more healthful ways. It's exciting to see so many young people taking part. I know many of them go home and cook for their families, which is great. One inspired person can change a whole family's dining habits.

My nephew Carlos Moore (a soccer star who is already on his school's varsity team while in the eighth grade) brought me into the twenty-first century by naming the most popular sedentary activities of teens and preteens these days.

Many of the youth summer campers were interviewed, and some are quoted in the following pages. They provide wonderful insights into cooking and gardening.

My twin nephew and niece, John and Mackenzie Moore (both avid athletes at age nine), suggested their favorite recipes using vegetables from their garden in Fairfield, Connecticut. Thanks to them we have Green Beans with Mustard Sauce (page 83) and Homegrown Carrots with Yogurt Ranch Dressing (page 112).

My dear friend Katie Stagliano, of Katie's Krops fame, contributed her grandfather's Eggplant Parmesan (page 70), a classic eggplant preparation. We home gardeners can't have too many eggplant recipes in our repertoire.

The University of South Carolina President's House is never a quiet place. I thank Dean of Libraries Tom McNally for providing me with secret writing places.

We host about two hundred events a year in the President's House and garden, but the activity really picks up when I have a book in the works. Many thanks to Joyce Taylor, housekeeper, and her assistant, Sharon Williams. Both women keep the house looking put together even in the midst of fairly consistent chaos.

Lisa Robinette is the President's House manager and associate director of special events for the University of South Carolina. Lisa has superb organizational skills, squeezes my calendar to get more than twenty-four hours out of each day, and is so thoughtful that we are never out of milk when we return from a trip. I couldn't organize my life without her. She makes everything manageable and every event beautiful.

Pam Bowman, director of special events, ensures that the most minute detail of every event is perfect. She promotes my interest in decor from the natural world—simplicity and sustainability—and helps to ensure that our events are generally plant based and "low carbon impact."

Darek Tidwell, presidential catering chef, shared his most excellent nut-crust recipe for Nut-Crusted Creamy Almond and Fruit Tart (page 139). This one's a winner and so are his fish tacos!

Karen Rood is a wonderful editor. She has great ideas and even greater organizational abilities. If ever you retire, Karen, you must leave me your cell number!

Thanks to Pat Callahan and Brandi Lariscy-Avant for art direction and layout. I can still feel the thrill of the first time I held *Greek Revival: Cooking for Life* in my hands. It is so beautiful and professionally done thanks to Pat and Brandi.

I can't say enough positive about Jonathan Haupt, director of the University of South Carolina Press. When *Greek Revival: Cooking for Life* was published, I neglected to acknowledge him because his work promoting the book had just begun. He was then assistant director for marketing. He did a fabulous job in that role and has since been promoted to director. He is an intellectual and a man of great integrity. We are confident that he will take the University of South Carolina Press to new heights.

Let me also thank the new marketing director, Suzanne Axland, for all the effort she *will* invest in getting *Greek Revival from the Garden* out to the world.

Finally a most special recognition to my wonderful husband of thirty-two years, Harris Pastides. (Okay, you'll have to indulge me here.) Harris, your love sustains me. Your encouragement has always made me believe in myself. You've instigated a lifetime of exciting adventures for our family, especially the international journeys. You've inspired me to dream. I thank you. Now eat more vegetables!

Artichoke

Eating for Life

Why Food Choices Matter

FOOD SUSTAINS our bodies. Just as we put high-quality fuel in our cars to keep them running optimally, we need to fuel our bodies with nutritious food. There are many foods to choose from. Some are more effective than others in maintaining high performance, so it's good to know a few nutrition facts in order to choose the best foods for energy and health.

Our bodies use *carbohydrates, fats,* and *proteins* for energy. And they require *vitamins, minerals,* and *water* in order for them to be used properly. For an overview of your body's nutritional needs, read on. . . .

CARBOHYDRATES

"Carbs" are the required energy source for the brain, keep our organs functioning, and provide energy for physical activity. About 45–65 percent of our daily diet should come from carbohydrates. It is important to know there is a wide range of carbohydrate types, and not all carbohydrates will improve our health. For simplicity we'll call them "good" and "bad" carbs.

Good carbs—including whole fruits, vegetables, and whole grains—have lots of nutrients and fiber, and many are low in calories. Certain foods, such as beans and lentils, are rich in both carbohydrate and protein, making them super healthful. These foods—along with whole grains such as oats—are digested slowly and keep our bodies feeling full longer. The beans, fruits, and vegetables you harvest from your garden will offer "good carbs."

Bad carbs are processed foods that are low in fiber, calorie intense, and nutrient poor. Think of "junk foods" such as doughnuts, sodas, and chips. Highly processed grains—such as flour used to make white bread, cakes, and pastries—fall into this category too. Bad carbs are digested quickly, sending a spike of sugar to your blood and making you feel hungry sooner.

It's best to choose carbohydrates that are good sources of fiber because it has been shown to protect us from many health problems. Fiber helps to

CARBOHYDRATES THAT ARE GOOD SOURCES OF FIBER

- lentils
- artichokes
- dates
- beans
- berries
- whole oats
- parsnips
- greens
- pears

prevent constipation; overweight; prostate, breast, and colon cancers; gallstones; and heart disease.

FATS

Eating unsaturated fats from plant sources and fish is essential for the health of every cell in our bodies. No more than 30 percent of our daily diet should come from fats. Certain fats called *essential fatty acids* are necessary to maintain life; others ensure optimal functioning of our organs. These *good* fats are especially required by the nervous system and are associated with emotional well-being. Good fats help to reduce chronic inflammation and otherwise improve biological functions, thus helping to prevent diseases such as cancer and heart disease. They are also important for healthy skin and bones. Here's the scoop on good fats and bad fats.

Many *unsaturated fats* are good. They are derived from fruits such as olives and avocadoes; vegetables such as canola (rapeseed), soy, corn, and sunflowers; nuts of all kinds; and fish, especially oily cold-water fish such as wild-caught salmon. These fats are satisfying to eat and beneficial to our health. They have even been shown to keep us from becoming overweight. Choosing unsaturated fats from a variety of sources is important for ideal health. It is easy to get these good fats through liquid oils such as extra virgin olive oil (the favorite of the Traditional Mediterranean Diet—TMD) and canola oil. Unsaturated fats provide an efficient source of stored energy for the body.

Saturated fats are not essential in the diet. Our bodies can make such fat from carbohydrates. Mainly coming from animals, saturated fats are found in products such as meats, cheeses, nonskim milk, and butter. Saturated fats have been most strongly linked to heart disease. Some popular foods containing unhealthy fats are hamburgers, bacon, hot dogs, fried chicken, cheesecake, and ice cream.

Trans fats have been shown to be extremely unhealthy and should be completely avoided. They are basically unsaturated fats that originate in liquid form and are then processed by hydrogenation into solids. Trans fats include stick margarine and solid vegetable shortening (often used to make pie crusts).

Trans fats are usually found in processed foods such as crackers, cookies, and cakes. If you're craving a sweet, it's preferable to make one at home. Tart crusts can be made without trans fats and with a minimal amount of butter; they can be filled with fruits and berries (see the recipe for Nut-Crusted Creamy Almond and Fruit Tart on page 139). Cakes can be made with canola oil. The TMD includes lots of fresh fruit for dessert, so—better yet—go to your yard and pick a few figs!

Broccoli is an excellent source of vitamins C and K and a good source of vitamin A.

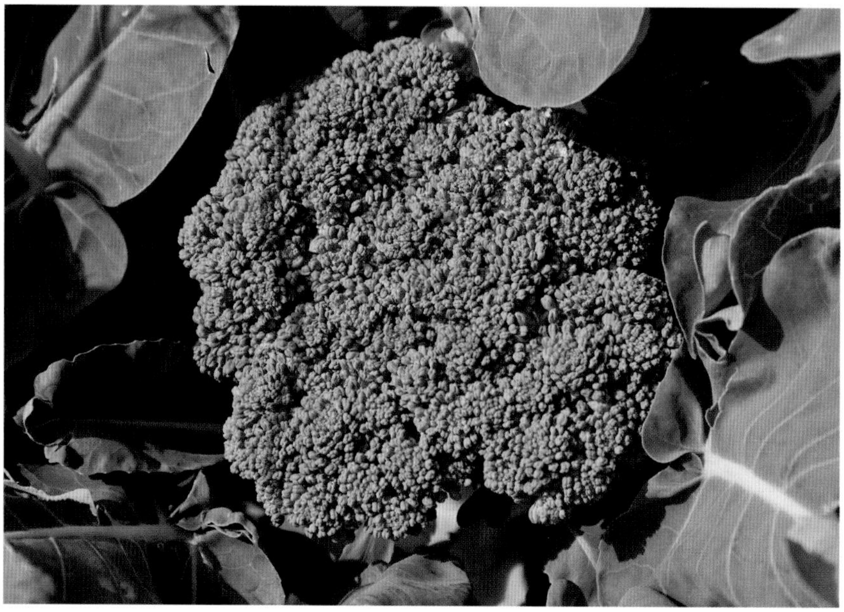

PROTEINS

Proteins have two roles: they help to build muscle, cell membranes, and hormones required by our bodies to stay strong, grow well, remain healthy, and feel emotionally balanced, and they provide fuel. Ten to thirty percent of our daily diet should come from protein. Proteins come from both animals and plants.

Animal proteins are found in meat, fish, eggs, cheese, and yogurt. *Vegetable proteins* come from beans, nuts, tofu, whole grains, and quinoa (a small seed that cooks like a grain). Scientific research shows that people who eat fewer animal products have lower blood pressure, less heart disease, and less cancer than people who eat more meats and cheeses. It's good for the body to utilize proteins from a combination of fish and vegetable sources such as beans, lentils, sesame seeds, and nuts. Quinoa provides a complete protein for humans. If you want to derive complete proteins from beans, eat whole grains too. Fortunately we have lots of delicious whole grains available today, including barley, brown rice, oats, and bulgur (par-cooked whole wheat that is then dried and crushed).

VITAMINS

Vitamins are natural substances created by plants, which our bodies need to grow, develop, and utilize energy contained in the carbohydrates, proteins, and fats we consume. Fruits and vegetables are great sources of vitamins.

Dark-green, leafy vegetables such as kale and spinach contain *vitamin K,* which works in the body to clot your blood when you get cut. (Let's hope this won't happen in the kitchen!)

Vitamin C is in all citrus fruits, including oranges, lemons, and grapefruits, as well as in cherries, kiwis, and vegetables such as bell peppers, broccoli, and Brussels sprouts. Vitamin C strengthens your body's immune system, which works to keep you healthy when you're exposed to germs and helps in healing wounds.

Vitamin A (including *provitamin A*)—in sweet potatoes, carrots, kale, butternut squash, spinach, and collard greens—is important for good vision and skin. It also supports a strong immune system.

Vitamin D is important for the development of strong bones because it stimulates calcium absorption. Mushrooms are one of the few vegetables that contain vitamin D, but it is also in some of the "fatty fish" such as tuna, salmon, and mackerel—foods common in the TMD.

The sunshine you will get while gardening allows the body to make its own vitamin D. Because of the risk of skin cancer, however, too much exposure to the sun is not recommended. It's a good idea to read more on this subject and decide what's best for you. I limit my sun exposure to twenty minutes during the morning hours between nine and eleven and avoid the sun between noon and two. If I need to be outside for longer periods of time, I use sunscreen with an SPF of at least 15 and wear a large-brimmed hat. I use a higher SPF on my face, ears, neck, and shoulders, which are more likely to burn—or I use it all over if I know I won't be able to resupply sunscreen while I'm outside. My large-brimmed crushable hat has become part of my typical "uniform" in the garden. Remember that sun damage you acquire in your teen years will become the precancerous (or even cancerous) lesions you will have to have removed when you are middle aged. That being said, I personally believe in prudent, short exposure to morning sunshine as part of a healthful lifestyle.

There are at least seventeen different vitamins our bodies need to function well, grow, and repair themselves when needed. If one of these crucial nutrients is absent from our diet, health problems can arise.

MINERALS

Our bodies require small quantities of various minerals, inorganic elements naturally present on the earth. Minerals are found in soil and water. Plants absorb them, and in turn humans acquire essential minerals by eating fruits and vegetables and some animal products, such as meat, fish, milk, and yogurt.

Calcium and *magnesium* support bones and teeth. In the TMD the richest sources of calcium are yogurt, sardines, and dark-green leafy vegetables such as turnip greens and kale. Magnesium is present in many TMD foods, including bulgur and other whole grains, almonds, nuts, spinach, black-eyed peas, beans, and lentils.

Iron is important for healthy blood. Without enough iron the body becomes fatigued, and the ability of the immune system to fight off infections and diseases decreases. Spinach, lean meats, poultry, fish, eggs, and nuts are all good sources of iron found in the TMD.

Potassium is very important for healthy blood pressure; it also keeps muscles strong, supports the nervous system, and promotes the healthy working of our kidneys. The TMD provides many good sources of potassium, including potatoes, beans, beet greens, butternut squash, raisins, and spinach—most of which you can grow in your own garden.

You are probably already aware that *fluoride* helps to prevent dental cavities. Most public water supplies in the United States are fluoridated. Fluoride is also available in sardines, other fish, and chicken.

There are several other vitamins and minerals that our bodies require to be healthy and fit. For more nutrition information consult the Academy of Nutrition and Dietetics, www.eatright.org. The easiest way to be sure that we are ingesting essential vitamins and minerals is to eat a large variety of the following foods:

- Colorful fruits and vegetables such as dark-green leafy vegetables (kale, spinach, arugula, beet greens, mustard greens, Swiss chard, collard greens, and cabbage), broccoli, Brussels sprouts, pumpkin, squash, carrots, sweet potatoes, red peppers, tomatoes, berries, apples, cherries, grapes, oranges, plums, bananas, and melons. Different colors in fruits and vegetables signify that the foods contain different vitamins and minerals required by our bodies.
- Beans, seeds, and nuts such as lima beans, white beans, lentils, black-eyed peas, navy beans, sunflower seeds, Brazil nuts, walnuts, cashews, almonds, and peanuts.
- Whole grains such as brown rice, oats, bulgur, and barley.
- Seafood such as shellfish, tuna, halibut, and wild salmon.

In short the TMD, if adhered to closely, has us covered!

WATER

You probably already know that our bodies are made up of 80 percent water. Water is a lubricant for our bodies and a very important constituent of each cell and organ. It needs to be replenished throughout the day. If you've ever had the experience of being dehydrated, you know exactly how much your body needs water. A long bike ride without water on a hot sunny day can be enough to cause a bad headache, a sign of dehydration.

A recent study by the Dole Nutrition Institute showed that participants who drank at least five glasses of water a day had half the risk of fatal heart disease than those who drank fewer than two glasses of water a day. In another Dole study, drinking about two glasses of water while exercising was associated with an increase in metabolic rate, which means that participants who drank water while exercising actually burned more calories than those who did not drink water. So, in addition to eating well and fueling our bodies with all the best foods, we need to be sure to drink plenty of water every day too.

CHOOSEMYPLATE

In 2010 the federal government began a campaign called ChooseMyPlate (see www.choosemyplate.gov) to help Americans know what kinds of food and what portions of those food groups make up a healthy diet.

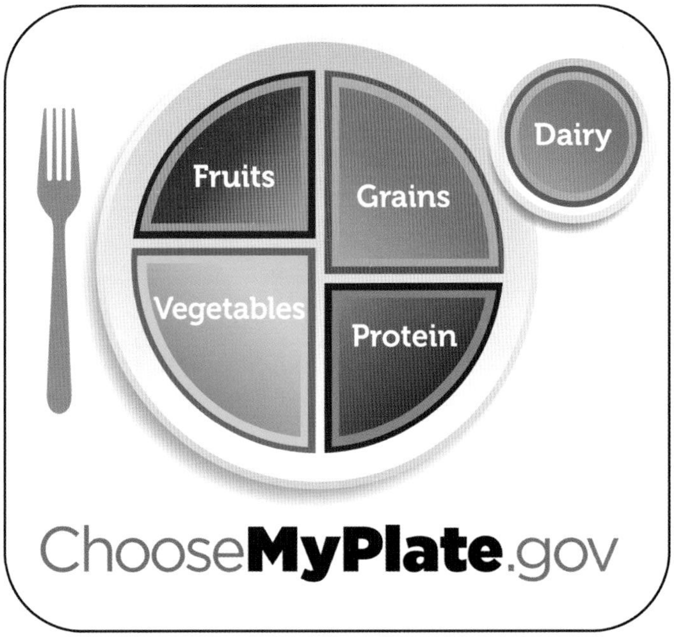

U.S. Department of Agriculture

The first thing we all need to consider is the size of our dinner plates. Back in the 1950s, the average size of a dinner plate was seven inches in diameter. Today dinner plates are more likely to measure ten or eleven inches. Before you even consider what foods should go on your dinner plate, measure it from one side to the other. If your plate is on the big side, remember that when you are filling it up and leave some room on the edges. Start with small portions. If you're still hungry when you've eaten those, you can always go back for seconds.

ChooseMyPlate shows us a way to be sure we are getting lots of fruits and vegetables and whole grains in our meals. The protein space might be for a bean dish, a piece of fish, or a meat stew. There are lots of healthy choices, especially in the TMD.

CHOOSING THE TRADITIONAL MEDITERRANEAN DIET

The TMD is recognized as one of the best diets in the world for promoting health and long life. It has been studied since 1958, and the results of the studies have consistently shown extensive health benefits, such as reduced risk of hypertension (high blood pressure), high cholesterol, inflammation, heart disease, stroke, cancers, Alzheimer's disease, diabetes, arthritis, childhood allergies and asthma, and age-related blindness.

Most Americans can name members of their families who have one or more of these illnesses. Some people think that, if their parents have a certain

CHOOSING MEATS FROM FREE-RANGE ANIMALS

Although meat is only occasionally eaten in the TMD, when we do, I feel it's extremely important to consume meat that has been raised in a healthful manner. In the same way that the human body is healthiest when we get exercise every day and eat a nutritious diet free of chemicals and processed foods, so too are animals' bodies healthiest when they are free to roam and run every day and eat the foods nature intended for them.

When I purchase meats, I buy them from local farmers whose animals are raised in this way and are not given antibiotics or growth hormones. I don't want to ingest such additives. The bonus is that I also get more flavorful meats that are naturally leaner.

disease, they will have it too, and there's nothing they can do about it. This is incorrect.

It is true that our genes can predispose us to a disease, but researchers are finding that our lifestyles can either "turn on" or "turn off" certain diseases. Even when we experience illnesses, our lifestyles can make them better or worse.

When we speak of "lifestyle," we are referring to our daily habits, how we live our lives. If we lead a healthy lifestyle, we *don't* use tobacco products; we *do* exercise each day for at least thirty minutes (even if it's just fast walking), and we *choose* a healthful diet, such as the TMD.

Drugs and alcohol are particularly potent and damaging to the developing brain and body, so young people should avoid them entirely. One to two small glasses of wine with meals in adulthood has been determined to be beneficial for otherwise healthy people who do not suffer from alcoholism.

What Is the TMD?

Let's start with what it's not:

- It's *not* popular "Americanized" versions of Greek or Italian food.
- It's *not* a "diet" in the sense of something you follow for a short period of time to lose weight.

The TMD is a way of eating for your whole life and includes the following:

- large quantities of fresh vegetables
- large quantities of fresh fruits
- beans and nuts several times a week, or daily
- whole grains daily
- moderate consumption of seafood
- extra virgin olive oil as the primary source of fat
- meats only occasionally
- dairy products in moderation
- moderate consumption of wine with meals

What makes the TMD so healthy?

- whole fresh fruits and vegetables (many colors = different vitamins and minerals)
- sources of fat (extra virgin olive oil = #1)
- *plant-based* sources of protein (beans, nuts, and whole grains = healthy fats without growth hormones or antibiotics)
- seafood = brain food

- *no* highly processed foods (which are filled with trans fats, corn syrup, artificial colors, and preservatives)
- time (Yes, you read that right!).

Time may be one of the healthiest attributes of the TMD. Read on. . . .

The TMD Lifestyle

Natural and unprocessed foods make for a healthy diet, but *how* we prepare and eat these foods is also important to health. We Americans lead a busy, fast-paced lifestyle. It causes us to eat on the run, to grab fast food and eat it in our cars. Many families no longer sit down to eat dinner together. In countries where the TMD is eaten, there has been a long tradition of sitting at the table with family and friends for hours, eating slowly, taking time, talking, and relaxing with a meal. You might not think this is important to health, but it is. Maybe it's the communication among family members that makes people feel happy and secure. Maybe taking the time to eat slowly allows our bodies to digest our foods better and to absorb the nutrients more fully. For whatever reason, this *relaxed* pace of life, especially taking the time to eat slowly, adds to the health benefits of the TMD.

If we compare the TMD lifestyle with our American dining ways, we find many differences. For one thing Americans eat in restaurants more often. Even when families try to choose restaurants that serve higher-quality food than fast-food chains, they are at risk for growing fatter. In fact studies have shown that the more frequently people eat in restaurants, the fatter they become. Just

SEASONINGS THAT MAKE FOOD TASTE GREAT

Here are some delicious seasonings to use instead of salt:

- lemon juice and lemon zest (the yellow part of the peel)
- dried oregano
- mixed dried herbs (such as herbes de Provence)
- fresh herbs such as mint, basil, thyme, rosemary, sage, parsley, cilantro
- sesame seeds
- fennel seeds

like many prepared dinners that are available in supermarkets, many restaurant meals contain too much salt. It is now believed that eating too much salt is responsible for illness among Americans. High blood pressure and stroke are associated with too much salt. These used to be conditions that affected only older people, especially the elderly, but today we see more and more children and young adults with high blood pressure and even having strokes. The TMD uses little salt. Instead it incorporates a large variety of fresh herbs and spices and fresh lemon juice to add flavors to foods—a much healthier (and tastier) approach.

Another difference between the American way of eating and the TMD has to do with how we feel after a meal. Have you ever felt as if you would burst after eating a super-sized fast-food meal but found yourself looking for a snack as soon as you got home? That's because our bodies burn some highly processed foods so quickly that we can feel overfull one minute and hungry a short time later.

The foods of the TMD will make you feel full and satisfied, and that feeling will last longer because the foods will fuel your body more effectively. By choosing the TMD, you can be assured that you are eating a balanced diet that gives you all the nutrients your body needs to be healthy and to work efficiently and effectively for a long life.

Good news: The TMD is easy and fun to prepare. The really good news: The TMD tastes great!

So what do we need to get started? A good, affordable source of fresh fruits and vegetables is essential. In communities all across America, there are farmers markets, roadside stands, and community gardens. Through a community-supported agriculture plan (CSA), your family can buy a share in a farm's crops. Probably the most economical and fun way to get great fruits and vegetables is to grow your own! Read on. . . .

Figs

Growing for Life

Getting Started on Your Garden

WHEN I WAS A TODDLER my father made me a picture book. It was called "Patricia's Tree." He drew all the pictures on card stock and stapled the book together. The first picture was of a small brown seed planted in an open green field. The seed grew into a sapling and then into a full and fabulous apple tree with pink flowers, red apples, and golden leaves according to the season. By winter it looked hopeless—gray and bare—but by spring it was once again abloom. I loved it so much I colored all over it. Today we have real fruit trees in our garden: figs, plums, pears, one pomegranate, and a few citrus. We also have lots of vegetables.

To me, starting with seeds and growing food feels like one of the most satisfying accomplishments in life. We have a long growing season here in South Carolina, and I'm thrilled week after week when I witness the new growth of colorful fruits, vegetables, and flowers.

Growing our own vegetables has also been a real inspiration for trying new recipes. We have a large garden, but you can grow vegetables just about anywhere that is sunny, even on your porch. Regardless of where you live and how much outdoor space you have, there is a way for you to get started growing your own vegetables.

THE ALL-IMPORTANT SOIL

Whether you garden in pots, a raised bed, or a yard garden, you will want the soil in which your plants grow, mature, and bear fruit to be as clean and nutritious as possible. A nutrient-rich soil, free of harmful chemicals and mixed to suit the type of garden you choose, is the foundation for your success.

Containers require a light potting soil while raised beds need a combination of topsoil and potting soil plus a small amount of organic matter, either mixed with yard soil or not. Topsoil and yard soil differ from source to source, and both should be tested for pH and available nutrients at your local extension office.

Soil is without question the most critical factor in the success of any garden. Rich soil infused with organic matter will foster a thriving garden.

COMPOSTING

One of the most satisfying ways to produce organic matter is by capturing the natural cycle whereby plants grow and take nutrients from the soil and then die and decompose, releasing nutrients back into the soil. Composting is nature's way of recycling. To create a compost pile, you can use all the spent organic matter around your home. Leaves that fall from trees, grass clippings from your yard, raw vegetable scraps from your kitchen, coffee grounds, and eggshells all add up to great nutrients for your soil.

WHAT TO PUT IN YOUR KITCHEN COMPOST BUCKET

- coffee grounds
- fruit and vegetable scraps, peelings, cores, and rinds
- eggshells
- nutshells

WHAT **NOT** TO PUT IN YOUR KITCHEN COMPOST BUCKET

These items might attract rodents or promote disease:

- all cooked foods
- meats
- fish
- bones
- dairy products
- pet waste
- raw eggs

The most nutritious compost results from a mix of green and brown plant materials. Kitchen vegetable scraps, grass clippings, and green plant matter such as prunings are the green group. The brown group includes fallen leaves, branches, and pine straw. Chopping or grinding the materials can speed decomposition.

As the contents of your compost pile decompose, the process creates heat, which accelerates decay and kills pests, diseases, and weeds. It is important to turn the compost material with a pitchfork at least once a month to let in air, which also speeds up the process of decomposition.

In a warm climate, such as that of South Carolina, it takes about three months for a huge pile (say three cubic feet) of compost material to decompose into a dark-brown powdery material that smells earthy (not stinky) and can be used instead of commercial fertilizer to enrich your soil. In colder climates the process will take longer.

Some people throw vegetable peels and scraps right in their garden without composting them. This is not recommended because, as they decompose, the vegetable scraps and peels actually take nutrients (nitrogen) from the garden soil.

The compost bins we constructed from wood pallets

HOW TO COMPOST

Locate a spot near your garden or raised bed where you can have two fairly large sections for your compost. Each one should measure about a cubic yard (three feet deep by three feet wide by three feet tall). It's good to have two so you have plenty of room for all your yard and kitchen scraps. It also gives you more room to move the more decomposed material toward the outside and the more intact material toward the center of the pile.

Wood pallets make a great frame for a compost bin because they have spaces between their boards, allowing good air circulation to help break down organic matter. There is no need to dig a hole for your compost pile; just set the wood pallets into the earth on three sides to frame your bin, leaving the front open so you can easily add to or work on the pile.

You can also make a compost frame from bales of straw. See the instructions at About.com/Organic Gardening, organicgardening.about.com/od/howtocompost/a/How-To-Make-And-Use-A-Straw-Bale-Compost-Bin.htm.

Some commercial outdoor compost containers are available as well.

Rake up fallen leaves, lawn clippings, or tree and bush prunings, chop them up a bit, and put them into your outdoor compost area.

Place a covered bucket in a convenient location in your kitchen and collect fruit and vegetable peelings, cores, and trimmings—as well as coffee grounds and eggshells—in it. Empty this kitchen compost bucket into your outdoor compost area daily.

TOOLS FOR GARDENING

You don't need to buy out the garden center to start a garden. Here are the basic tools you will need:

Sunscreen and a hat with a large brim

Garden gloves

Shovel

Pitchfork

Trowel

Hard-tooth rake

Hoe

Hose

Water wand

Watering can

Wheelbarrow

Rototiller (optional)

Turn the material in your compost area with a shovel or pitchfork routinely to accelerate decomposition. When the material in your bin is fully composted, it should be dark brown, crumbly, and not smelly.

Use the composted organic matter as you prepare your planting beds or garden. Rake it into the soil before sowing seeds or planting seedlings. You can also add more around the plants as they grow. If you have enough composted matter, you can spread it on the ground throughout the garden as mulch (see below). If not, you can put some shovelfuls at the base of plants and work it into the existing soil. Your plants should look very green and healthy, and you should begin to see worms enjoying your nutrient-rich soil. Whether you garden in containers, raised beds, or a yard garden, remember to add organic matter to the soil every year to replenish your precious soil.

For general composting information see the Clemson Extension Service website, www.clemson.edu/extension/hgic/plants/other/compost_mulch.

MULCH

Wherever you garden it is a good idea to spread a protective covering called "mulch" on the soil. Mulch holds moisture in the soil, keeps weed seeds from germinating, and moderates soil temperatures. Organic mulches such as straw, pinestraw, half-rotted leaves, or wood chips slowly decompose in place, adding organic matter back into your garden.

Watering a raised bed

WATERING

Wherever you plant, make sure your garden is well watered. A good rule of thumb is to keep the soil slightly damp at all times—not soggy and not dry but always *evenly moist.*

If leaves look limp, you may have waited too long to water. Many plants will recover from occasional neglect, but withholding water too often will stress your plants over time.

Too much watering can also make plants look wilted. That's because the roots have rotted from being too wet or because the roots are so saturated with water that they can get no oxygen and can no longer deliver water to the plant. At that point your plant may be beyond saving.

Watering after sunset may promote fungal growth on plants because the lack of sunshine and cooler evening temperatures mean the water stays on the leaves longer. It's generally thought that the best time to water is in the early morning.

Additional, specific guidance for watering containers, raised beds, and yard gardens is included in those sections.

Some vegetables, such as this tomato plant, need stakes, cages, or trellises to help them grow upward and not topple over. Other plants that need support include eggplants, peppers, pole beans, cucumbers, and peas.

CONTAINER GARDENING

A container garden is one where you grow your herbs and vegetables in large pots or other receptacles. A collection of pots can line your steps or the walkway leading up to your door. Pots can brighten up a fire escape or bring life and color to your back porch.

Sunlight

You can grow many vegetables and herbs in containers and some fruits as well. Most vegetables need a lot of sunshine, five to six hours per day, so it's best to place your containers in the sunniest space you have, but there are some vegetables that grow in partial shade. All herbs like full sun too, but some—such as chives, cilantro, mint, parsley, and thyme—will grow well enough for a kitchen garden in partial shade.

Shade-Tolerant Container Vegetables

Vegetables that will grow in pots with limited sun exposure include:

- arugula: 3–4 hours of sun per day
- Asian greens such as bok choy or totsoi: 2 hours per day
- chard: 3–4 hours per day
- kale: 3–4 hours per day
- lettuce: 3–4 hours per day
- mesclun: 2 hours per day

- mustard greens: 3 hours per day
- spinach: 3–4 hours per day.

Basic Steps

After finding a sunny spot for your containers, and before you begin planting, place them where they will stay. Containers can get extremely heavy when they are planted, so it's easiest to place them first.

Make sure your pot has drainage holes. Fill the pot with soil. For containers you need a light soil that doesn't pack down densely. "Potting soils" (which don't actually contain real soil) are good. Many of these mixes contain pine bark, vermiculite, perlite, and sand. Such mixes are a good choice for container gardening. For your container gardens, never use topsoil or a soil mix that feels heavy when you lift the bag.

Plan out where each plant will go before beginning to plant the container.

Plant the herbs or vegetables at the same depth they were in the small pots they came in.

Add a bit more soil until it reaches to about one inch below the rim of the container. You will want this remaining inch when you water the container.

Water the plants thoroughly.

Watering and Fertilizing

The biggest job for container gardeners is watering. In the heat of the summer you may need to water your containers twice a day. All this watering can take the nutrients out of the soil. You might want to add a bit of compost from time to time as a sort of "multiple vitamin" for your soil. You can use your own organic compost, mushroom compost, or any of the composted animal manures. Fish emulsion is readily available and can be used to give the soil a quick nutrient boost. It is fast acting but not overwhelming to the soil. Compost and fish emulsion are organic means of replenishing the soil in your pots without harming your seeds or delicate seedlings.

Using Fish Emulsion

To apply fish-emulsion fertilizer:

- Dilute the fish emulsion according to package directions.
- If you are growing plants from seeds, apply the diluted fish emulsion directly to the soil in the pot when the second set of leaves emerges on the plant stems.
- If you start out with plants, apply the diluted fish emulsion on the first planting day.

- Reapply the diluted fish emulsion approximately every three weeks after the first application.

Containers

When choosing containers, remember that, as plants grow, their roots need to spread out, so you might like to start with containers of a good size (around ten to twelve inches). Make sure your containers have drainage holes in the bottom so the roots don't sit in water.

If you have to go out and buy some containers for your garden, try clay containers that are unglazed. They breathe better than glazed or plastic containers, and plants do better when air circulates, cooling the soil in the heat of summer. Since clay pots allow the soil to dry out more quickly, you will need to water more often. If you have perfectly good plastic containers, you can certainly use those because a good soil mix should promote air and water circulation. Pots need lots of water especially as the season progresses.

For fun you can recycle other containers to grow smaller kitchen herb gardens. We recycle all our olive-oil cans as mini herb gardens. They do well outdoors or in a sunny window, and after you use the herbs, you can always plant more. When it's time to change the herbs, it's best to compost the old plants and soil, wash out the container, and then pot the new plant in new soil. This will keep your kitchen herb garden fresh.

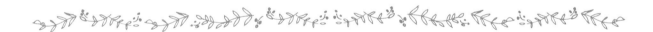

A CONTAINER HERB GARDEN

- Remove the top of an empty 1-gallon olive-oil can with a can opener.
- Wash out the can, being careful of sharp edges.
- Poke 4–6 holes in the bottom of the can using a manual punch can opener.
- Add potting-soil mix and composted fertilizer (see Basic Steps, page 20).
- Plant 2–3 seedlings of fresh herbs such as basil, thyme, rosemary, chives, and oregano in the can.
- Keep your mini herb garden in a sunny place, water as needed, and trim the herbs for cooking.

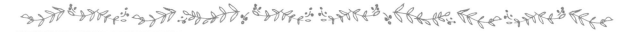

A SALAD BOWL

Lettuce grows well and quickly before the weather gets too hot. This is a wonderful spring container project because you can enjoy lettuce before most other vegetables. The lettuce mix, radishes, and cilantro in this garden do best in full sun.

Arrange the lettuce and cilantro seedlings in the center of the container, leaving a bit of space between them. Plant the radish seeds around the plants as a border. When the radish seedlings grow to about two inches, thin them out if necessary, selectively removing some of the plants to allow others to grow.

Keep the pot well watered.

When you harvest lettuce, keep it growing by clipping the outside leaves. The central core will sprout new leaves.

Supplies:

- a bowl-shaped container, 6–8 inches deep and 18 inches in diameter, with drainage holes
- potting-soil mixture (as described under Basic Steps, page 20)
- compost fertilizer (straight from your compost bin)
- fish-emulsion fertilizer (see Using Fish Emulsion, page 20)
- 1 four- or six-pack of lettuce seedlings (European mesclun mix is colorful and provides several flavors from mild to lemony to spicy.)
- 1 packet of radish seeds (Plant only one-third of the seeds at a time.)
- 2 cilantro seedlings or 1 cilantro plant
- 1 nasturtium or pansy plant (edible flowers to make your salad elegant!)
- sunlight
- water

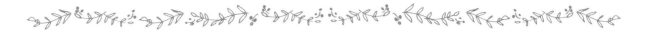

A PIZZA GARDEN

Plant and water your seedlings and/or seeds according to the directions on the plant sticks or seed packets.

You can't grow pepperoni, but you'll love your pepperoncini!

Supplies:

- a large container, about 30 inches tall and 24 inches in diameter, with drainage holes
- soil mix (see Basic Steps, page 20)
- compost fertilizer
- fish-emulsion fertilizer (see Using Fish Emulsion, page 20)
- 2 cherry tomato plants and 2 small stakes to stabilize them
- 1 oregano plant
- 1 basil plant
- 1 pepperoncini plant
- sunlight
- water

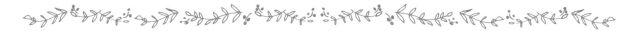

AN HERB-POT TOWER

If you'd like to have a tower of herb pots, here's how to make one:

- Take a ½-inch diameter piece of rebar that's about 6 feet tall.
- Wearing your garden gloves and using a large-headed mallet, hammer the rebar into the ground about 18–24 inches. Ask for help if you need it.
- Take 5 pots of varying sizes, each with a center hole in the bottom. Starting with the largest pot, slide the rebar pole through the hole in the pot bottom. Then tip the pot to one side so its rim rests against the rebar. Continue to stack the pots in this way, leaning them in various directions to create a whimsical appearance. Finish with the smallest pot, tilting it to hide the top of the rebar pole.
- Fill the pots with soil and compost.
- Plant herb seeds or seedlings in the pots. Basil or rosemary should be planted in the larger pots at the bottom because their roots need more room to spread.

Oregano, sage, and parsley would be good choices for the middle pots.

Chives would do best in the top pot because they need less water than the other herbs.

Don't forget to water!

RAISED BEDS

If you have a sunny outdoor space but most of your yard is devoted to flowers, trees, bushes, and maybe a playground area or pool, you can consider gardening in a small raised bed. Because it is raised off the ground, this kind of garden plot is a contained area that won't spread, and you may be able to make it more pest resistant than a traditional garden. A raised bed may be built with wood that is nailed together to create a frame, or it can be made from stones or bricks or even an old bathtub!

Raised beds on the University of South Carolina campus before they were planted in spring 2012

Here are some ideas for making a raised bed:

- Find a sunny spot for the bed, preferably a place that enjoys six hours of sun per day.
- With the help of a skilled family member or friend, build a frame with wood, stacked bricks, or stones. Make this frame at least twelve inches tall. The width should be at least one foot but no more than three to four feet, so you can reach into the center of the bed to tend to the plants. Cedar is a good choice for the frame because it is more resistant to rot than other woods. Pressure-treated lumber lasts a long time, but many gardeners are concerned about the chemicals from the lumber leaching into the soil and contaminating the vegetables. Some people use pressure-treated lumber and line their raised bed with a thick plastic tarp to protect the soil from perceived chemical exposure.
- Your raised bed can be on your lawn or in a rocky area. The easiest method of raised-bed gardening is to cover the area of lawn within your frame with a padding of newspaper about one-half inch thick. This will prevent grass and weeds from growing into the bed. Then add your soil on top of the newspaper.
- Or using a shovel, you can till (turn over) the lawn in the bed area so that the soil from your yard can be mixed with new soil you will add to the bed. This way the plants' roots can grow more deeply and establish themselves

The raised beds flourishing

well into the soil. Make sure to remove any grass or weeds from the soil so they won't grow in your garden. You can throw the grass or weeds right into your compost pile (see pages 14–18).

- Fill the bed with soil. You can use a blend of topsoil and potting soil. Spread the new soil you add to the bed with a rake, and if you have tilled under your lawn instead of covering it, rake the new soil into the native soil so they blend, which will allow the plants' roots to anchor better. Add organics for nutrients. These organics can be from your own compost of grass clippings, decomposed leaves, and vegetable scraps, or organic matter that you purchase, such as mushroom compost or composted animal manures. Animal feeds such as alfalfa meal and beet pulp also make good fertilizers. Add a two- or three-inch layer of compost material or other fertilizer and blend it into the soil mixture. Lightly water it before you plant.
- Next plan what vegetables you would like to plant. Consult your local extension service, and/or experienced gardeners in your area to decide what varieties to grow and when it's safe to plant them outdoors.
- Next decide how you will arrange your vegetables. Read the seed packets and seedling sticks to determine how to space the seeds and seedlings. Following these directions is important. Some plants grow very bushy, so you won't want to plant them too close together. You might want to draw your plan on a piece of paper.
- Plant the seeds at the depth indicated in the seed-packet instructions, and plant the seedlings at the depth they were planted in their original containers.

- Mulch the bed with straw, pine straw, or newspaper. These materials will hold the moisture in the soil and suppress the growth of unwanted weeds. Plus it's another great recycling opportunity!
- Water the bed thoroughly. It is important to check your raised bed often to make sure it gets enough water.

YARD GARDENS

Because long hours of sun exposure are best for growing fruits and vegetables, the first step in planning a yard garden is to find a nice sunny spot where you have at least six hours of sunlight each day. If possible, try not to plant your garden in a low spot. It might stay too wet, which would not be healthy for your vegetables. It is also best not to plant a garden too close to a tree because you might find yourself having to fight shallow tree roots, which will invade the garden once you've enriched the soil.

Another consideration is having a water source and your compost nearby. You will need to cart water and organic matter to the garden, so having close access to both is important to think about as you plan your garden. Don't forget to create paths that lead to a hose and the compost. You should plan for paths within the garden too. You will need to walk through the garden to weed it and to pick the produce without stepping on the plants.

Consult your local extension service, and/or experienced gardeners in your area to decide what crops will do well in your climate and when the ideal

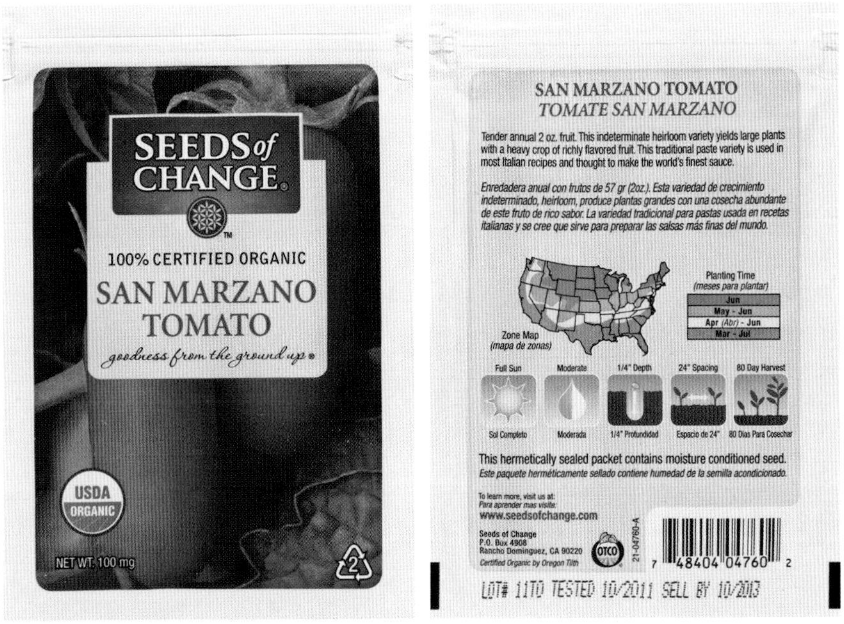

A typical seed packet with information about planting, germination, and growing conditions

time to plant them will be. Most of the vegetables you choose will have to be planted every year, but if you are planning to have fruit trees or berry bushes you will need to find permanent places for them to grow. You won't want to move them. I have a wall at the back of my garden where the fruit is clustered. I started with two fig trees that looked like skinny sticks, and by the second year they had grown to about seven feet tall by six feet wide. Remember to plan for growth. That is the goal after all!

Most fruit trees are also beautiful. They flower in the spring and have colorful foliage in the fall, so you might like to plant your fruit trees in a place of prominence in your yard.

When planning your garden, you have the choice of planting the vegetables in single rows or in blocks. With block planting you plant four or five of the same plant across and perhaps four or five down so you have a square of one plant. If plants are concentrated in blocks there is less opportunity for weeds to germinate among them. That's the good news. But if you live in a hot, humid climate, block planting can prevent air circulation, promote fungus, and attract insects. It may also make watering evenly more difficult as plants' leaves grow, creating a cover over the soil.

Individual rows of plants will have paths between them and will promote better air circulation. You will easily see each separate plant so you can spot pests and signs of diseases that might be present. We hope they won't be there for you to see!

SOLARIZATION

Because it doesn't require much digging, *solarization* is a simple measure for killing grass and weeds, controlling fungal and bacterial soilborne pathogens (germs), and improving the nutrients in the soil so it is ready for planting a vegetable garden. If you're starting a raised bed or garden in your yard, you can prepare the soil by solarizing it. This method works best in warm, sunny climates and during the hottest weeks of the year.

- Rake up any debris from the area where you want to locate your garden.
- Water the area well.
- Stretch a clear plastic tarp across the area to be solarized and secure it firmly all around so that the wind won't pick it up.
- Leave the tarp in place for 4–6 weeks.
- Remove the plastic and plant away!

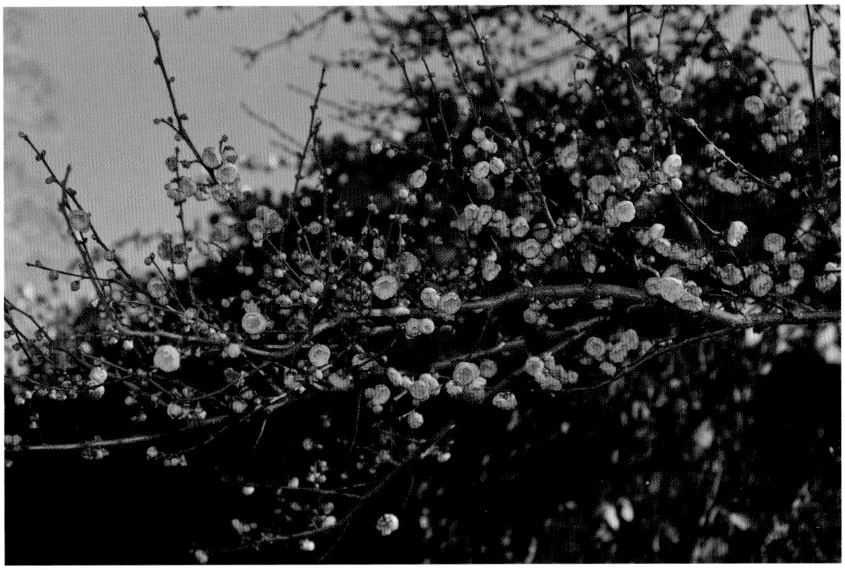

A flowering apricot tree in our garden

Unfortunately, when sunlight hits the paths in a garden planted in rows, it creates a welcoming environment for weeds. To avoid weeds you can put some straw down on the paths.

As with containers and raised beds, you need to read about how large your plants are expected to grow, so you can plan how closely together to plant them.

If you're like me, when the mood strikes you to garden, you'll be so excited that you'll want to plant all your vegetables at once. This may not be the best plan.

Take leaf lettuce for example. If you sow all your lettuce seeds on the same day, you'll have your lettuce harvest all within about four to five weeks. This is fine if you want to give lettuce to all your neighbors or to a local food bank. But you could also sow a third of the seeds, wait two weeks and sow the second third, and then wait another two weeks to sow the final third. Instead of having all your lettuce at once in four to five weeks, you'll have the first lettuce in that amount of time and continue to have lettuce for about three months.

Some seeds take longer to germinate than others. If you interplant fast-growing seeds among slower ones, you'll see some results sooner. This approach to planting leaves less room for the weeds to take over. For example radishes are fast growing, so you might want to plant them among carrots or parsnips, which are slower growing. Fast-growing lettuces will let you explore green salads while you wait for the tomatoes and peppers planted nearby.

An example of block planting

Different varieties of the same vegetable often mature at various times in the season. By choosing different varieties of tomatoes for example, you can harvest tomatoes for a much longer period of time than if you grow just one variety. This holds true for figs, blueberries, raspberries, and many other fruits. If there is one vegetable that you really enjoy, check out a seed catalog to see about its varieties and their yield times. (You can request free seed catalogs online.)

Another thing to think about is what to grow next. When your early vegetables are all harvested, you can pull up those plants and plant other vegetables. Depending on your climate, you can plant and harvest potatoes early in the season. After you've dug them all up, you can add more compost material to the soil and plant tomatoes or sweet potatoes in the same space. Here's a guide to starting a yard garden:

- Read the following directions before you begin. They may help you decide what size garden you'd like.
- Identify part of your yard that gets the most sun (at least six hours per day).
- Have your soil tested to be sure it does not contain lead or other dangerous contaminates. Call your state department of health and environmental control or a local university extension service to determine the easiest way to get your soil tested.
- Decide on the size of your garden and mark its boundaries with stones or stakes.
- Remove all grasses and weeds from your garden plot. They will not be wasted if you put them into your compost bin, where they will break down and eventually become your fertilizer. Using a long-handled shovel with a pointed blade, cut sections of earth and then scoop off the top layer, which holds the grass. This can be dumped in a wheelbarrow and taken to your compost site. Just be sure to break it up into chunks in the compost. Don't worry, you're building your biceps!
- If you have light or sandy soil, dig the soil with a shovel to loosen it up. If you have very dense, dry, or clay soil you might want to use a rototiller (see tools, page 17) to till the soil and lighten it so you can dig. This can be a big time saver. Rototillers can be rented, but be aware they can be dangerous. If you don't have access to a rototiller, don't worry. Schedule a "garden party": invite all your friends to bring rakes, hoes, shovels, or pitchforks, and serve refreshments in exchange for their help!
- Add composted organic matter (or soil amendments as suggested for raised beds, page 26) evenly over the area and then rake or shovel them

together with the soil. You will want loosened, fertilized soil that is about ten to twelve inches deep.

- Plan and mark off paths to your water source and compost area and throughout the garden for harvesting your crops.
- Plan what vegetables you want to grow. Consult your local extension service or experienced gardeners in your area to decide what crops will do well where you live and in what season they will flourish.
- Next plan where you want to grow each crop, and using a hoe, dig a small trench in the soil to make a row. If you've done a good job of enriching your soil, your plants will get bigger than you think, so don't crowd the rows.
- Water lightly down the length of the row.
- Bend down and carefully sow your seeds or plant your seedlings along the row using the depth and spacing recommended on the seed packets or seedling sticks.
- Carefully top the seeds with the soil you have set aside and a little more composted organic matter; lightly tamp it with the top of the rake. In the case of seedlings, plant them as deeply in the earth as they were in their small pots, then surround them with additional soil and compost matter, gently packing the soil around the plant to provide stability.
- Make sure to leave a label at the end of each row or part row so you will be able to identify what is growing there. Seed packets tend to blow away or fade in the sun and water, so it's best to make more permanent signs.
- To prevent birds from bathing in your newly loosened soil and digging up the seeds, use straw, newspaper, or cardboard to protect the rows. Don't use a thick layer of material, which might smother tender seedlings as they begin to grow, but something organic around them will deter weeds and help to maintain moisture. The material will break down in the sun and rain and with watering over time. Use only light straw on plants that are fast growing—such as lettuce, which takes only one week to germinate. Also use only straw on seeds that are sprinkled for block planting. You may surround other seeds or seedlings with newspaper or cardboard to hold moisture in the soil and discourage weeds. These materials should never be placed directly on top of seeds or seedlings.
- Water your newly planted garden. Pay close attention to the watering needs of your plants. Seeds and seedlings are sensitive to too much water, so follow directions for watering carefully. A watering wand attached to a hose long enough to reach all areas of the garden plot works well. As with any type of garden, watering after sunset is not recommended.

A recently planted yard garden shows rows don't have to look boring.

Leaf lettuce

Be patient, but get excited! Check your garden daily, water when needed, and enjoy watching small seedlings grow strong and green shoots sprout from seeds. The wonders of nature are astounding.

PESTS

Vegetables sometimes attract pesky insects that will munch on leaves, slugs and snails that will bore holes in cabbages, and birds that will peck at figs and out-and-out steal blueberries. All the creatures of the natural world love a garden. Plant enough to share! Here are a few tips to cut down on your disappointment:

- Plant a variety of crops. If insects are targeting one crop, you'll still have others.
- Plant flowers in and among your fruits and vegetables. Flowers attract many kinds of beetles, butterflies, and insects that will prey on garden pests. Marigolds deter a wide variety of insects and beetles, so they are a good flower to plant near potatoes, tomatoes, eggplants, and peppers. Nasturtium flowers and leaves are beautiful and edible, and they repel aphids, squash bugs, whiteflies, and pumpkin beetles—so plant them near beans, cabbages, and cucumbers.
- Fruit trees and blueberry bushes can be covered in mesh netting to keep birds out. Once in a while you might have to let a bird out of the net. They have a way of finding their way in when the fruit is ripe!

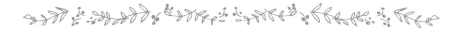

MULCH: HAY OR STRAW?

Hay and straw are not one and the same.

Hay is a tall field grass that is cut down whole—seed heads, leaves, and stalks—and left to dry in the sun. It is then baled and used for animal feed. Never use hay for mulch because the seeds in it will sprout, and you'll have weeds in your garden.

Straw is the hollow stems of grains such as wheat, barley, and rye, which are left over after the seed heads have been harvested. Straw makes a good mulch. It will discourage weeds from growing and improve the soil as it decays.

- Bright yellow plastic cups covered in Vaseline and resting on sticks near your plants will attract whiteflies and aphids away from your vegetable plants. You can never catch them all, but this method does help.
- Slugs and snails like beer, so if you find them tearing up your cabbage, lettuce, or pepper plants, leave shallow dishes of beer next to your vegetables, and they'll crawl into the beer instead of munching your vegetables.

Gardening Advice: Plant your favorite things! Then choose some vegetables that you think you don't like or have never tasted and plant as many of these as you have space for.

MY FAVORITE THINGS: CHOOSING VEGETABLES TO GROW

Finally we're ready to think about what to grow!

You may be a person who eats lots of vegetables and fruits, or someone like Julia, a twelve-year-old aspiring actress who claims to be a vegetarian but doesn't really like vegetables. Her friends all chime in that she's really a "carbovore." Apparently Julia eats a lot of noodles. Yet she does like cucumbers, carrots, and most fruits, so that gives her a starting point.

You're about to learn how to cook the TMD way. Having lots of fruits and vegetables to choose from is like being an artist who has many, many colors of paint and a canvas that stretches across yards. Here are some good choices:

HERBS: basil, rosemary, thyme, sage, mint, oregano, chives, parsley, dill

FRUITS: strawberries, blueberries, raspberries, watermelon, cantaloupe, Meyer lemons, figs, pears, plums

VEGETABLES: cucumbers, carrots, potatoes, sweet potatoes, spinach, zucchini, broccoli, cabbage, beets, parsnips, peas, beans, onions, garlic, tomatoes, radishes, Brussels sprouts, eggplant, lettuces, kale, Swiss chard, butter beans, peppers

Don't forget sunflowers, which are beautiful and exciting—and their seeds are nutritious for our bodies and our soil!

One last gardening reminder: when you choose which vegetables you want to plant, investigate how much room they will take up. One type of cucumber plant might cover twenty-five to thirty-five square feet, while a bush cucumber will need only four square feet.

Onward to the kitchen!

Cooking for Life

Getting Started in the Kitchen

IF YOU'RE NEW TO COOKING, there are some basic things you need to know about navigating your kitchen. First of all, there are dangers lurking in those drawers and cabinets. Probably the most obvious hazards are sharp knives (though dull ones have their way of being a menace too) and hot stoves. Before we jump into cooking, let's consider how to avoid getting hurt in the kitchen. It's also important to consider personal hygiene and safe food-handling practices so we avoid spreading germs that can lead to food poisoning or other illnesses. Finally I'll list equipment needs and introduce some cooking terminology so you'll be prepared to create the best-ever TMD feast for your family and friends.

SAFETY FIRST: BEWARE OF HOT, HEAVY, AND SHARP OBJECTS

Since there are hot, heavy, and sharp objects in the kitchen, talk with your family about guidelines for cooking in your home before you get started.

If you are cooking with your family, there's a lot you can learn. Many students I interviewed during cooking classes at Columbia's Cooking!, an interactive community cooking program offered through the Cancer Prevention and Control Program of the University of South Carolina's Arnold School of Public Health, started cooking with their parents or grandparents. In her first cooking class, ten-year-old Caroline suggested: "Always watch your parents, since they've been cooking longer."

A University of South Carolina student cooking class featured our campus-grown cabbage.

The "bear claw" method of chopping protects your fingertips.

I've found that the most important ingredient in every recipe is the attention the cook brings to the preparation. Staying really focused in the kitchen is important. Taylor, a sixteen-year-old girl helping out in a cooking class for younger students, offered this advice: "Be careful, don't get sidetracked, and don't speed through recipes. Cooking takes a lot of patience." And an experienced ten-year-old named Alysha, who has attended three week-long summertime cooking camps, agreed: "Keep your eye on the food at all times, never walk away."

Cooking is both creative, like an art project, and exacting, like a science experiment. As in any activity you care about, you have to know and follow the safety rules, know the equipment and techniques, give your undivided attention to what you're doing, and do your best. Preparing a meal can be as fun and rewarding as painting a landscape or being part of a robotics team. Let's look at some common safety concerns in the kitchen:

Knives

To avoid cutting yourself, choose a knife that is right for the job. Different kinds of knives are shown in the equipment list (see page 41).

Make sure your hands are clean and dry before you begin cutting. Water or olive oil on your hands can make you lose control of the knife.

Never cut anything while holding it in your hand. Always place the object to be cut directly on a clean cutting board and slice or chop it there. Hold it

Fast meals are a must for university students. Here we're making Sautéed Greens with Garlic over Pasta (page 76).

down on the cutting board with one hand and hold the knife in the other. Keep the fingertips of the hand holding the food out of the range of the knife blade. You can do this by curving your fingertips slightly under the first knuckle of your fingers, making a "bear claw" (see page 37) with your fingers while your thumb steadies the food. When you bring the knife down to cut, it will be guided by your knuckles and your precious fingertips will be tucked out of the way.

Wash each knife right after you use it. There are two reasons to do so: it will be clean if you need it to cut another ingredient, and you won't drop it into a sinkful of soapy water with other used cooking tools, where it might stab you later when you reach into the sink to wash the dishes.

Other Sharp Objects

Large graters used for shredding cheese are also very sharp. If you're not attentive you might grate your knuckles, which is not recommended for your recipe or your hand!

Microplane graters or zesters used for grating nutmeg or shredding the outer part of the rind from citrus fruits can be very sharp as well. When grating any food, make sure that you are holding a large enough piece of it to keep your skin from contacting the grater.

Food-processor blades are extremely sharp, so be very careful how you handle them when you insert and remove them from the processor and when you wash them.

Stovetops and Ovens

When using the burners on the top of the stove, make sure the area around the stovetop is clear. When you place a pot or pan on a burner, some of the heat can be deflected to the side, and if anything flammable is too close to the flame or heating element, it can catch on fire.

If you are using a gas burner, you will see the actual flame. When you turn it off, the flame will disappear, and the burner will cool down fairly quickly. If you have an electric stovetop, however, the burner will stay quite hot for a while after you shut it off. Many, but not all, electric stovetops now have red-light displays to remind cooks that the burners are still hot.

Most people are instinctively aware not to touch a flame or hot burner, but please note that another burn risk when cooking on the stovetop is steam. If you are boiling water for pasta for example, you must be careful to lift the pot lid away from you, thus directing the steam that way too. When you drain cooked pasta in a colander, be sure to hold your face away from the steam.

Another good tip is to keep the handles of the pots and pans on your stovetop pointed to the side or back of the work area. This way you won't accidentally knock the pots over and possibly burn yourself or someone else with boiling liquid or hot food.

When using the oven—before you turn on the oven to preheat it—make sure nothing is stored in it and that the racks are situated as the recipe directs.

Always use pot holders when handling pots and pans on the stove or in the oven. If your pot holder has gotten wet, use another one. Wet pot holders will not prevent you from being burned.

Finally, when checking food that is cooking in the oven, use pot holders to pull the rack toward you and then wait a few seconds before leaning toward the pan. Sometimes we get overly excited to see if a dish is done, and we lean in too far and too fast—and singe an eyebrow! Also remember that the inside of the oven door gets hot too.

Our middle-school students reminded us to wash our hands again if we touch our faces or heads or put our fingers in our mouths.

Heavy Objects

Roasting pans and *pasta pots* may be no problem for you to handle when they are empty, but it can be a real struggle to tote them when they're filled with food or water, and they are dangerous when their contents are hot. Make sure you know your strength before lifting hot and heavy objects.

Stand mixers and *food processors* can be heavy as well. Take care when moving them around in the kitchen.

Whatever you want to lift, ask for help when you need it.

SAFE FOOD HANDLING

To avoid accidental injury or unknowingly spreading germs while cooking, you should follow these rules for safe food handling:

- Wear closed-toe shoes.
- Tie back long hair.
- Wear an apron.
- Take off rings and watches.
- Roll up long sleeves.
- Wash your hands well with warm soapy water before you begin and after handling eggs, meats, and seafood.
- Remember to wash cutting boards with soap and water after each use.
- Make sure your kitchen surfaces are clean before you begin, and clean up as you go.

WASHING GARDEN PRODUCE

I generally "wash" all garden fruit, vegetables, and herbs by rinsing them with cool to tepid water.

I scrub root vegetables with a moistened, clean kitchen towel and rinse them under warm water.

It's useful to soak lettuce and greens in a bowl of tepid water to release any unseen dirt, insects, or worms. Then rinse the leaves under cool running water, and spin them in a salad spinner to dry them.

After rinsing herbs, I usually dry them with a clean kitchen towel.

Remember to wash fruits with warm water and a clean kitchen towel, especially if you will eat the skin, such as the zest of lemons and oranges.

If you compost the vegetable peelings and eggshells, throw away the meat trimmings, and recycle the packaging materials as you go, your kitchen will remain organized and easier for you to clean as you cook. These are the best tips to avoid spreading germs.

GREAT THINGS TO KNOW

To avoid disappointment, read the whole recipe before you begin. Make sure you have everything you need and time to make the recipe. There's nothing worse than starting a project and having to stop to run to the store, or having to leave everything because you have a practice or rehearsal to get to.

When using recipes for baked goods such as breads, cakes, cookies, and tarts, it's important to follow the directions in the recipe *exactly* to be sure what you're baking turns out well. Baking involves chemistry.

Many other recipes—and most of those in this book—are more like guides. After you follow them and make a dish successfully a few times, you will feel comfortable becoming creative and substituting different herbs, spices, or vegetables. In many of the recipes, I offer ideas of other ingredients that can be substituted. Once you get confident in the kitchen, you'll have lots of fun creating your own recipes. Adelaide, age twelve, cooks for her family of five every Wednesday night. She knows the power of creation in the kitchen: "I don't think cooking would be that fun if you only made what you know you like." Her favorite creation incorporated chicken and peaches baked in filo dough! Her family loved it!

Follow the recipe carefully. Jacob, who is eleven, liked the spinach pie he made in class. He said, "The filo dough was intimidating at first, but the recipe told us exactly how to use it. It's not that difficult, it's not rocket science!" In his household the kids take turns making dinners on Saturday nights and get paid ten dollars! "I might make spanakopita (spinach, feta, and dills pies) this Saturday night," he added as he finished the last bite, "it's not that hard!"

EQUIPMENT NEEDS

Cutting board

7¾-inch chef's knife

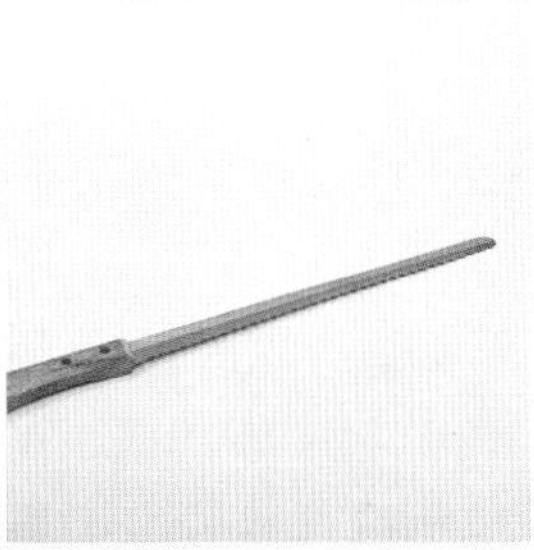

Serrated bread knife

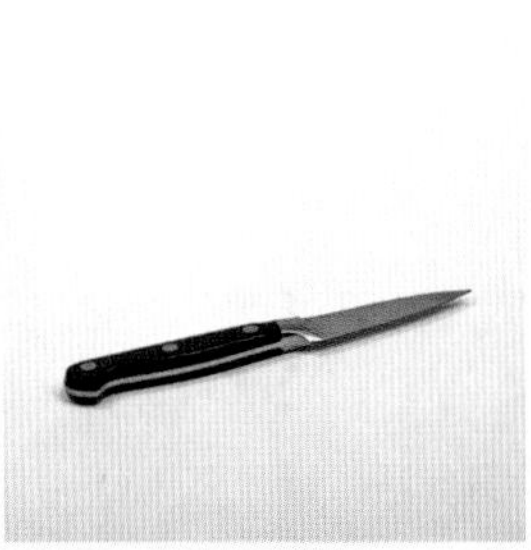

3-inch paring knife

Fish knife

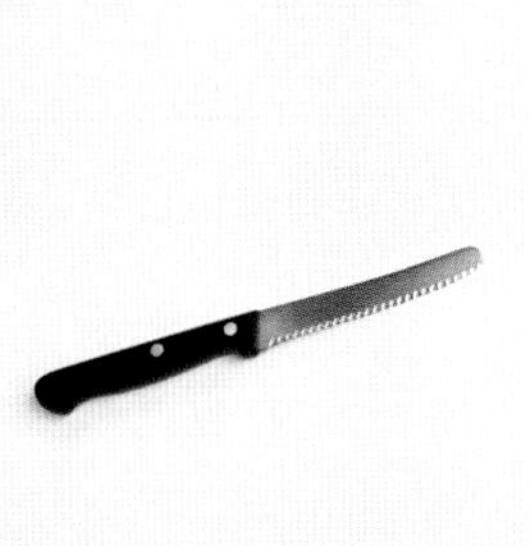

Tomato knife

Skewer

Colander

Fine-mesh sieve

Salad spinner

Sauté pan

Large sauté pan

EQUIPMENT NEEDS (continued)

Baking sheet with sides (jelly-roll pan)

Stockpot

Saucepan

Cast-iron enamel covered casserole

Food processor

Whisk

Mixing bowl

Stand mixer

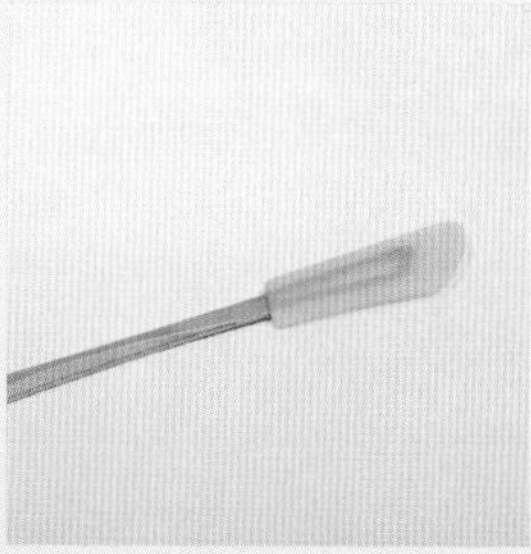
Rubber spatula

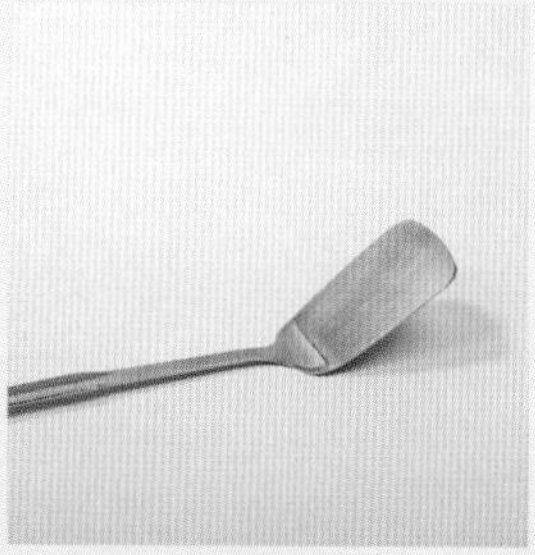
Metal spatula

Vegetable peeler

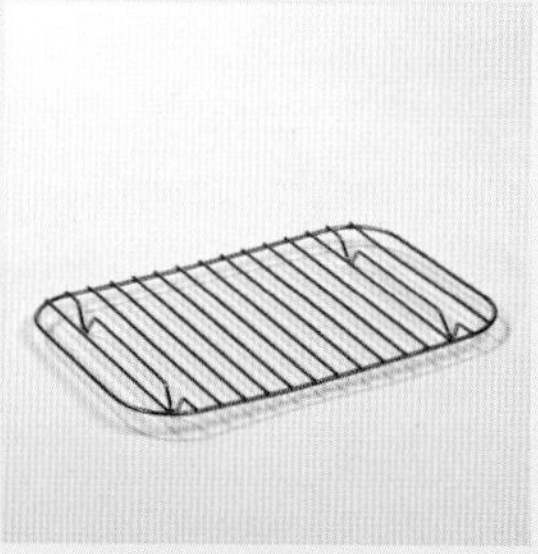
Wire cooling rack

Liquid measuring cup

Dry measuring cups

Measuring spoons

Roasting pan

Bundt pan

Cake-tester broom

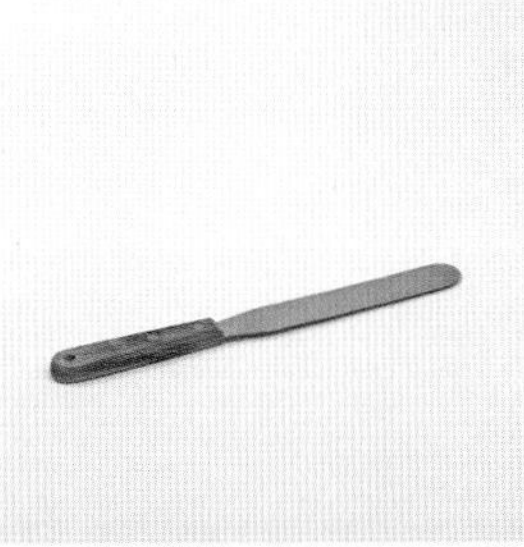

Frosting spatula

Metal slotted spoon

Wooden spoon

Wooden slotted spoon

Garlic press (mincer and slicer)

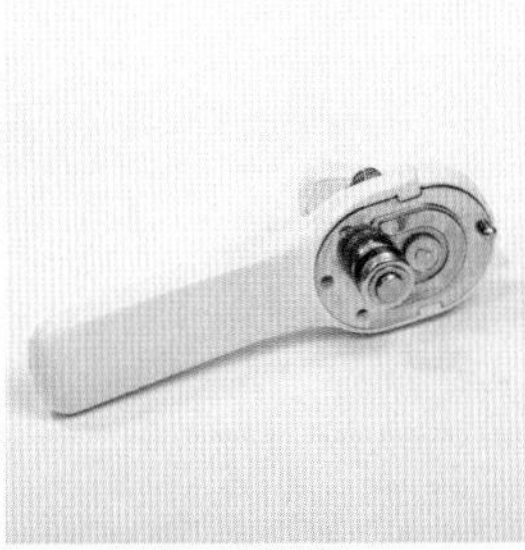

Can opener

Orange juicer

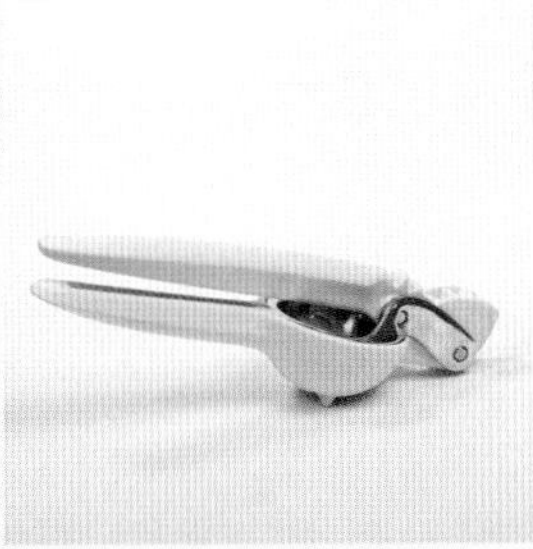

Lemon juicer

Basting brush

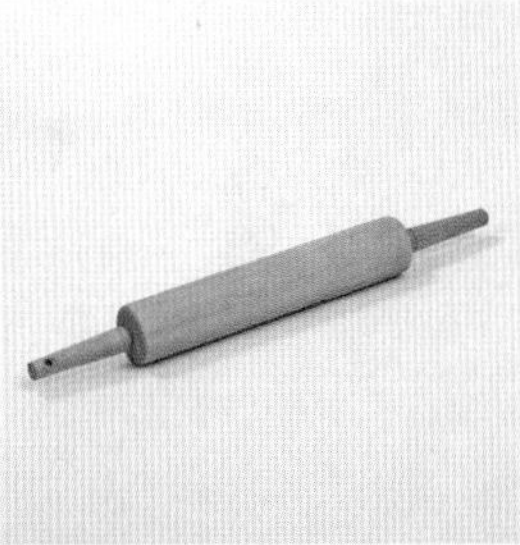

Rolling pin

Pizza stone

Trivet

Tart pan

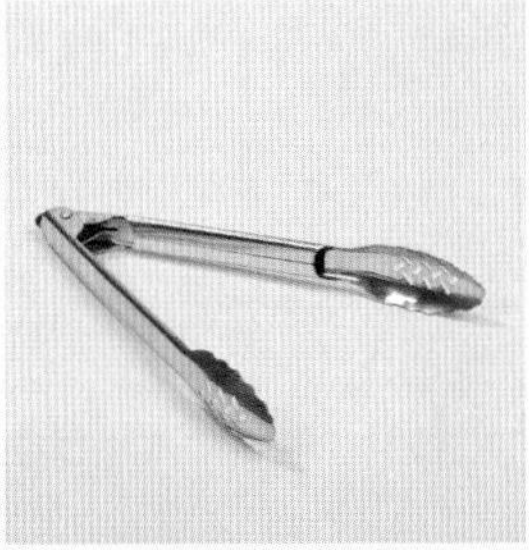

Tongs

EQUIPMENT NEEDS (continued)

Kitchen compost bucket

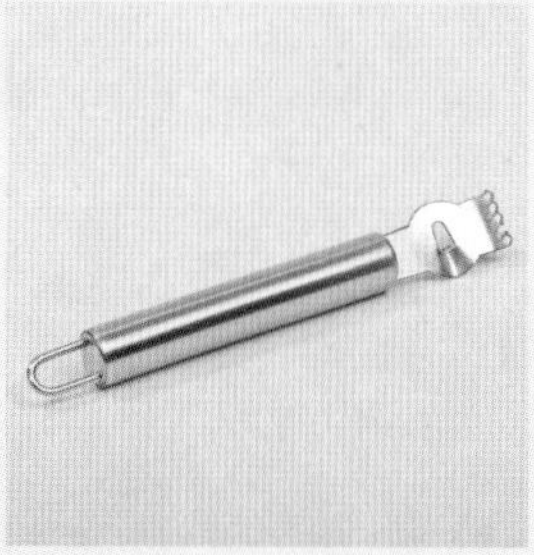

Zester

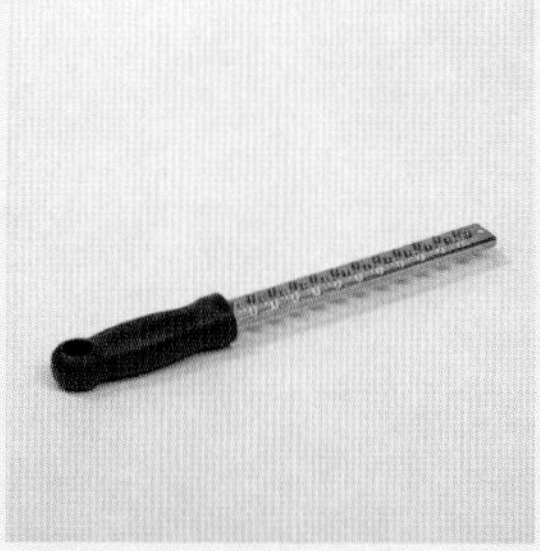

Microplane grater

Pizza cutter (pizza wheel)

Broiling pan

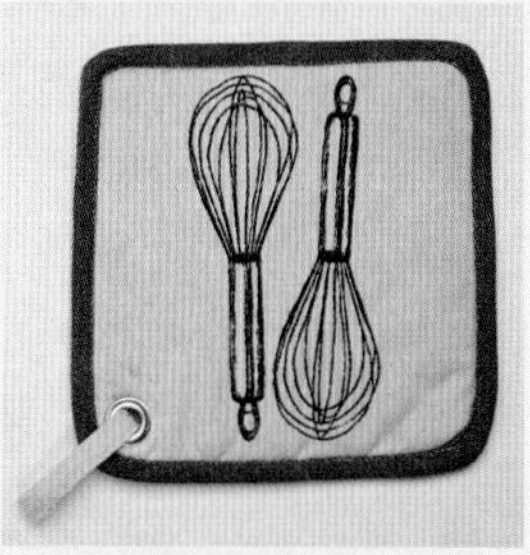

Potholder

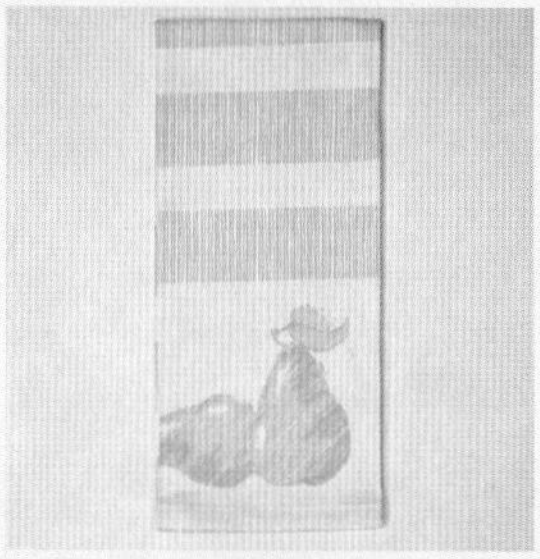

Kitchen towel

COOKING TERMS YOU SHOULD KNOW

Baking and roasting take place in the oven with the heat source on the floor of the oven; in the convection mode heat is circulated by a fan in the rear of the oven. The recipes indicate which type of baking or roasting should be used and where the pan should be placed in the oven.

Blanching is submerging fruits or vegetables in rapidly boiling water for a short period of time, usually followed by shocking, which means placing them in an ice bath to stop the cooking quickly.

Broiling occurs in the oven of an electric stove or in a separate compartment of a gas stove, usually below the oven. In both cases the heat source is located at the top. Generally with broiling one places the oven rack close to the heat source to create a sort of indoor grilling. A special broiling pan has a slotted tray atop a shallow pan designed to catch drippings from broiling meats.

Caramelizing, strictly speaking, refers to cooking sugar until it browns. But in the TMD I use it to mean cooking fruits and/or vegetables until the water in them evaporates and their flavors are intensified. Often they become brown, as in the cherry tomato recipe on page 48.

Convection baking or roasting is an oven setting that circulates the heat within the oven to distribute it evenly around the pan. If your oven doesn't provide a convection mode, use traditional bake or roast mode. The cook time may be a bit longer, and you'll have to turn the ingredients so they'll brown on all sides.

Crudités are thinly sliced raw or blanched vegetables.

Dicing is cutting foods into small cubes.

Grilling generally refers to outdoor cooking over high heat, which sears the meat and vegetables, making them brown and crispy on the outside. Some cooktops also have grills.

Julienning is slicing foods into thin strips.

Marinating is soaking a food in a dressing to impart flavor or tenderize it before cooking.

Mincing is tiny dicing.

Reduction involves cooking the liquid off a dish to make it thicker.

Rolling boil occurs when a liquid is heated until it is bubbling vigorously.

Sautéing is browning food on a cooktop in a pan with low sides (a sauté pan or frying pan). Start by heating a little extra virgin olive oil in the bottom of the pan and then add the ingredients. You can sauté quickly or slowly, but usually the heat should be on at least medium. You need to watch what you're sautéing and stir it around occasionally so that it won't burn. Generally speaking this cooking method keeps foods moist.

Simmering is allowing a dish to cook at a constantly low boil, usually to reduce the amount of liquid in it.

Vinaigrette is a dressing made of extra virgin olive oil and vinegar, usually with dried or fresh herbs added.

Zesting is removing part of a fruit skin (usually an orange or lemon peel) by using either a microplane grater, which creates the equivalent of minced pieces, or a zester, which cuts the skin into tiny threads or strips. Because the white pith part of the peel is quite bitter, you should avoid cutting into it. This is the reason special tools are made for zesting.

Classic Caprese Salad, page 57

Pulido-Walker Olive Oil produced by University of South Carolina alumna Donna Walker; label designed by Chas Pulido at age twelve.

Your Harvest Is the Star

Fifty Recipes

Tomatoes

Oven-Roasted Cherry Tomatoes with Balsamic Vinegar and Lemon-Thyme Confetti

- 1 pint cherry tomatoes
- 1½ tablespoons extra virgin olive oil
- 3 teaspoons balsamic vinegar
- ½ teaspoon sea salt
- ½ cup lemon-thyme leaves

Equipment: colander, clean kitchen towel, medium-sized bowl, baking sheet with sides, measuring spoons, cutting board, chef's knife, pot holders, spatula, serving dish

Preheat the oven to 375 degrees.

Put the tomatoes in a colander and rinse them in cool water. Dry them with a clean kitchen towel.

Place the tomatoes in a medium-sized bowl and drizzle them with the extra virgin olive oil. Using clean hands, rub the tomatoes in the oil until they are all lightly coated.

Add the balsamic vinegar and salt to the bowl and toss the tomatoes again until they are coated.

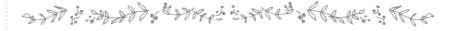

TOMATOES

For the best-tasting tomatoes, pick them just before you are ready to use them. Once you bring them into your house, store them in a cool, dry place, but never refrigerate them. Refrigeration will make their texture mealy and will rapidly destroy their flavor.

Place the tomatoes in a single layer on a baking sheet with sides.

Place the pan on the lower rack of the oven and bake the tomatoes for approximately 25 minutes, until they look wilted and their edges begin to turn brown.

While the tomatoes are roasting, remove the leaves from the lemon-thyme stems, pulling the leaves from the top down. They should slide right off the stems.

When the tomatoes are fully roasted, use pot holders to remove the baking sheet from the oven. Use a spatula or large spoon to transfer the tomatoes to a serving dish. Sprinkle them with the lemon-thyme leaves.

Serve immediately or at room temperature.

Serves 4

You can use fresh rosemary instead of lemon thyme. Pull the rosemary leaves from their stems and finely mince them as they tend to be fibrous.

Feta, Tomato, and Dried-Oregano Pizza

Equipment: cutting board, tomato knife, large sauté pan, measuring spoons, dry measuring cups, wooden spoon, large cutting board, pot holders, pizza stone, pizza cutter

- 2 tablespoons extra virgin olive oil
- 16 small plum tomatoes, chopped (about 4 cups)
- 2 teaspoons dried oregano
- ½ teaspoon sugar
- 8 ounces sheep's milk feta cheese
- 1 partially baked Whole-Wheat Pizza Crust (recipe on page 132)
- 1 teaspoon dried oregano
- ¼ cup fresh oregano leaves

Preheat the oven to 500 degrees.

Heat the extra virgin olive oil in a large sauté pan over moderate heat.

Add the chopped tomatoes and 2 teaspoons of oregano and cook them, stirring occasionally with a wooden spoon, until most of the liquid has evaporated from the tomatoes.

Lower the heat and continue cooking and stirring the tomato mixture a few more minutes, until it is quite dry. Remove the pan from the heat and crumble the feta cheese into the tomato mixture, stirring to combine ingredients.

Spread the feta-tomato-oregano mixture evenly over the partially baked pizza crust and sprinkle the topping with 1 teaspoon dried oregano.

Bake the pizza on a pizza stone in the oven for 8–10 minutes, until the crust is baked through and the topping is bubbling hot.

Using pot holders, carefully remove the pizza on the pizza stone from the oven. Slide the pizza onto a large cutting board and garnish it with fresh oregano leaves.

Let the pizza cool for a few minutes before slicing it with a pizza cutter.

Serves 4–6

The Purist's Chunky Tomato, Mozzarella, and Basil Pizza

Equipment: pizza stone, sharp knife, large wooden cutting board, large spoon, pot holders, pizza cutter

- 1 partially baked Whole-Wheat Pizza Crust (recipe on page 132)
- 1 recipe Chunky Savory Tomato Sauce (recipe on page 53)
- 8 ounces fresh mozzarella cheese
- 20 fresh basil leaves, roughly chopped

Preheat the oven to 500 degrees.

After removing your partially baked pizza crust from the oven, spread Chunky Pan Tomato Sauce evenly over the crust.

Using a sharp knife and a cutting board, slice the fresh mozzarella cheese into thin slices, about ¼ inch thick or less. (They don't need to match or be perfect!) Since fresh mozzarella is on the soft side, it can be a little difficult to slice.

Arrange the slices of mozzarella cheese on top of the tomato sauce.

Bake the pizza on a pizza stone in the oven until the dough is cooked through and the cheese is melted and beginning to brown, about 8–10 minutes.

Using pot holders, remove the pizza on the pizza stone from the oven. Slide the pizza onto a large cutting board and sprinkle the chopped basil leaves on top of the pizza.

Let the pizza rest for a few minutes before cutting it into wedges with a pizza cutter.

Serves 4–6

Chunky Savory Tomato Sauce for Pasta or Pizza

Equipment: large sauté pan, garlic press, wooden spoon, measuring spoons

- 3 tablespoons extra virgin olive oil
- 2 cloves garlic, minced
- 8 chopped Roma or plum tomatoes
- 3 teaspoons dried oregano
- 3 dried bay leaves
- ½ teaspoon sugar
- A sprinkle of red-pepper flakes (optional)
- ½ teaspoon sea salt
- Ground black pepper to taste

Heat the extra virgin olive oil in a large sauté pan over medium to medium-high heat. Cook the minced garlic just until it is light golden in color. Lower the heat if necessary to avoid burning the garlic.

Add the chopped tomatoes, oregano, bay leaves, and sugar and stir the mixture with a wooden spoon to combine. If you like a bit of heat, add red-pepper flakes to taste.

Let the sauce cook on a steady boil, stirring occasionally until the water from the tomatoes has been reduced by about two-thirds. If the sauce begins to stick to the pan, lower the heat. The sauce should not be completely dry, but it will be more savory when most of the water has evaporated. This sauce needs 15–20 minutes to cook depending on the type of tomatoes you use.

Season the sauce with ½ teaspoon of sea salt and a few grinds of black pepper.

Remove the bay leaves before using the sauce.

Serves 6 as pizza topping or 4 as a pasta sauce

Zesty Tomato, Kalamata Olive, and Seafood Bake

- 2 tablespoons extra virgin olive oil
- 1 large onion
- 4 ripe plum tomatoes
- ⅓ cup sliced pitted Kalamata olives
- 2 cloves garlic, peeled
- 1 cup dry white wine
- Juice of 2 lemons, about ½ cup
- 1 teaspoon fennel seeds
- 1 teaspoon dried oregano
- ½ teaspoon ground black pepper
- ¼ teaspoon red-pepper flakes
- 1 tablespoon extra virgin olive oil to brush on the bottom and sides of the baking dish
- 4 fish steaks (salmon, swordfish, or mackerel), each about 3–4 ounces
- 1 tablespoon lemon zest for garnish

Equipment: large sauté pan, cutting board, chef's knife, tomato knife, garlic mincer, liquid measuring cup, measuring spoons, microplane grater or zester, 9×11-inch baking dish

Preheat the oven to 375 degrees.

Heat the 2 tablespoons of extra virgin olive oil in a large sauté pan over moderate heat.

Slice the onion, add it to the pan, and cook it for about 5 minutes or until soft.

Chop the tomatoes (large dice) and add them to the onions.

Add the sliced Kalamata olives.

Mince the garlic and add it with all the remaining ingredients except the fish to the sauté pan.

Simmer the mixture over medium-low heat for about 15 minutes, stirring occasionally. If the sauce seems to be sticking to the pan, lower the heat.

Brush the baking dish with extra virgin olive oil and arrange the fish steaks in the dish so they do not overlap.

Pour the sauce from the sauté pan over the fish.

Bake the fish and sauce uncovered in the oven for about 14–15 minutes, until the fish is opaque and flaky when you insert a knife to check.

Serve immediately.

Serves 4

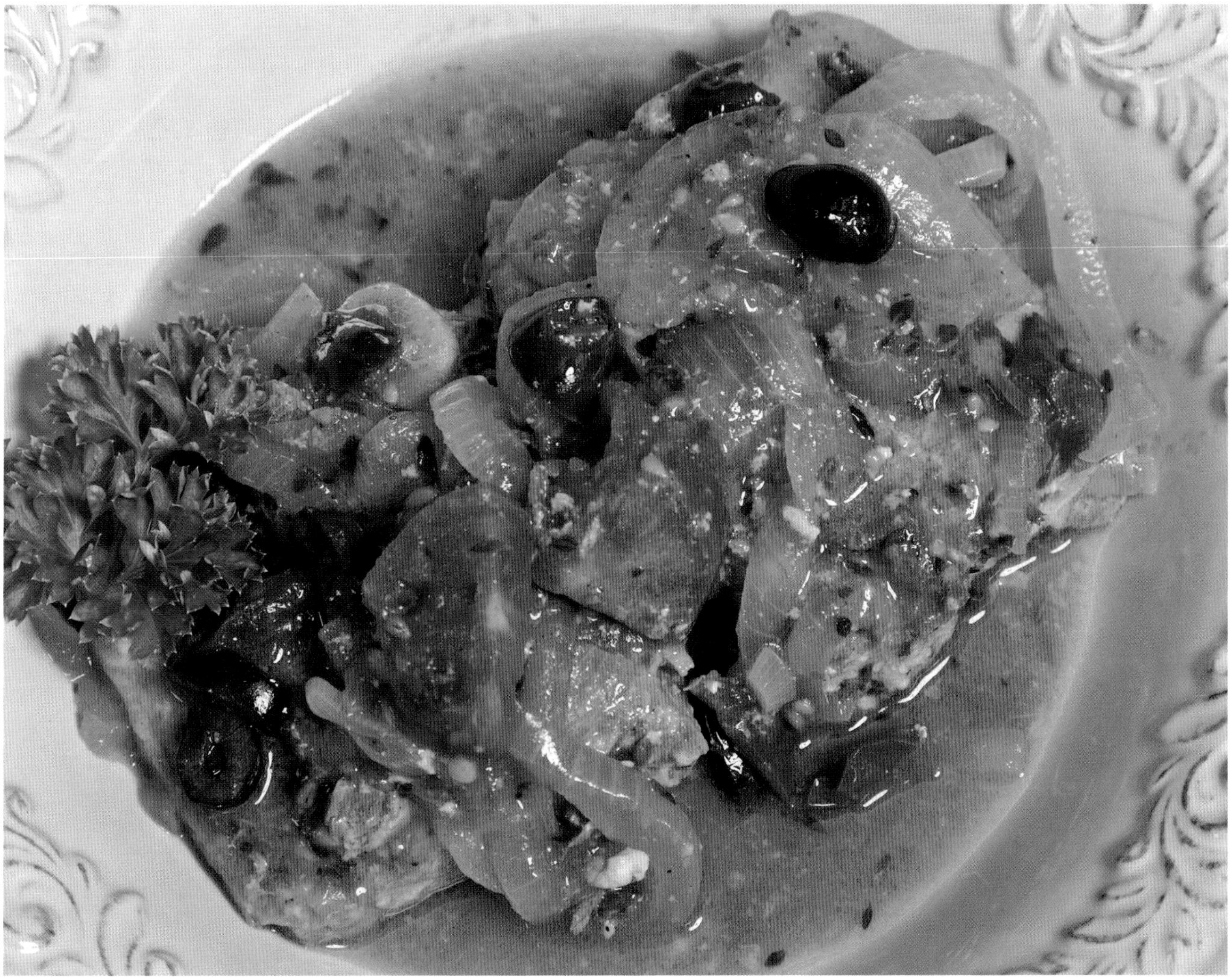

4 medium tomatoes
1 small red onion
1 small jalapeño pepper
2 cloves garlic, peeled
2 tablespoons fresh lime juice
½ teaspoon sea salt
½ teaspoon freshly ground black pepper
½ cup fresh cilantro leaves

Wash your hands after handling a jalapeño pepper as its juice can sting your eyes.

Tomato Salsa with a Kick

Equipment: cutting board, chef's knife, tomato knife, bowl, paring knife, garlic mincer, wooden spoon, measuring spoons

Finely chop the tomatoes and onion and put them in a bowl.

Finely chop the jalapeño pepper, being careful to discard the seeds and white spine from within. Add the jalapeño to the bowl of chopped tomatoes and onion, the "salsa."

Mince the garlic and add it to the salsa mixture.

Add the lime juice, sea salt, and ground pepper. Mix all the ingredients well with a wooden spoon.

Finely chop the fresh cilantro leaves and combine them into the salsa.

Serve immediately over grilled chicken or fish. For a vegetarian option add 1 cup of black beans and 1 peeled, pitted, and sliced avocado, and serve this salsa over brown rice.

Serves 4

Classic Caprese Salad

Equipment: cutting board, chef's knife, tomato knife, measuring spoons, dry measuring cups, serving platter

- 1 fresh mozzarella cheese, about 10 ounces
- 3–4 tomatoes, sliced into ¼-inch slices
- ½ cup small basil leaves (or large ones chopped)
- 2 tablespoons extra virgin olive oil
- Sea salt

Drain the mozzarella and slice it into ¼-inch slices.

Arrange the cheese and tomato slices alternatively, and overlapping slightly, on the serving platter. Place the basil leaves over the cheese and tomatoes. Drizzle with extra virgin olive oil and lightly sprinkle with sea salt.

Serve immediately.

Serves 6

Sometimes called buffalo mozzarella, this kind of mozzarella is usually sold in a container of whey or water in the delicatessen section of a grocery store or in a specialty cheese shop. It is very white and softer than the mozzarella that is grated onto pizza. It has a delicate flavor that blends well with tomatoes, extra virgin olive oil, and basil.

Garden Gazpacho

6 ripe medium-sized tomatoes
1 cucumber
1 red bell pepper
1 yellow (or green) bell pepper
1 small red onion
3 cloves garlic, minced
3 cups tomato juice
¼ cup red wine vinegar
¼ cup extra virgin olive oil
½ teaspoon sea salt
Freshly ground black pepper to taste
Fresh parsley, finely chopped for garnish
Thinly sliced avocado for garnish
1 jalapeño pepper, finely chopped (optional)
Crusty toasted bread

Equipment: cutting board, tomato knife, paring knife, chef's knife, teaspoon, liquid measuring cup, measuring spoons, vegetable peeler, food processor, garlic mincer, large bowl, wooden spoon

Wash all the vegetables.

Roughly chop the tomatoes and place them in the bowl of a food processor fitted with a steel blade. Pulse the food processor until the tomatoes are finely chopped, but not completely liquid. Pour the tomatoes into a large bowl.

Reassemble the food processor.

Peel the cucumber, cut it in half lengthwise, and scoop out the seeds with a teaspoon. Cut the cucumber into large chunks and process it in the food processor until it is finely chopped. Add the chopped cucumber to the bowl with the tomatoes.

Reassemble the food processor.

Cut the bell peppers in half, remove the stems, cores, and seeds, and cut them into large chunks. Place the chunks in the food processor and process until they are finely chopped. Add the peppers to the bowl with the tomatoes and cucumbers. (You can put the stems, cores, and seeds into your kitchen compost bucket.)

Reassemble the food processor.

Peel and quarter the onion. Place the pieces in the food processor and process them until they are finely chopped. Add the onion to the bowl with the tomatoes, cucumber, and peppers.

Mince the garlic and add it to the bowl.

Add the tomato juice, vinegar, extra virgin olive oil, salt, and a few grinds of black pepper to the bowl. Mix well with a wooden spoon.

Chill. Just before serving, garnish with parsley and/or avocado.

Serve with toasted crusty bread.

Serves 6

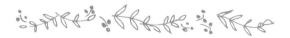

If you enjoy spice, you can add a finely chopped jalapeño pepper to the soup; just be sure to discard the seeds and the white spines before you chop it (as those parts of the pepper are very hot) and wash your hands when you are done.

Zucchini, Almond, and Mint Pesto over Pasta

½ tablespoon extra virgin olive oil
½ cup slivered almonds
3 medium zucchini
½ cup mint leaves (no stems)
2 cloves garlic, peeled
2 tablespoons chopped parsley
½ cup chopped blanched almonds
1 cup grated Parmesan cheese
⅔ cup extra virgin olive oil
1 pound whole wheat, or extra protein, pasta
Sea salt and freshly ground black pepper

Equipment: measuring spoons, small sauté pan, dry measuring cups, liquid measuring cup, wooden spoon, cutting board, chef's knife, teaspoon, pasta pot, slotted spoon, food processor, colander, serving bowl

Heat ½ tablespoon of the extra virgin olive oil in a small sauté pan over medium-high heat and cook the ½ cup of slivered almonds until they are browned. Remove them from the heat and set them aside to use as garnish for the finished product.

Halve the zucchini lengthwise and scoop out the seeds using a teaspoon.

Bring a pot of water (large enough for the pasta) to a boil.

Put the zucchini halves into the water. When the water returns to a boil, reduce the heat and simmer for about 8 minutes or until the zucchini is tender but still firm.

Turn off the heat and remove the zucchini with a slotted spoon. Save the water.

Place the zucchini, mint leaves, garlic, parsley, chopped blanched almonds, and Parmesan cheese in a food processor fitted with a steel blade and process them until the mixture is well blended.

With the food-processor motor running, pour almost all the extra virgin olive oil through the feeder tube and process until the oil is well incorporated.

Bring the zucchini water back to a boil and cook the pasta according to package directions.

While the pasta is cooking, taste the pesto; then season it with sea salt and freshly ground black pepper to taste.

When the pasta is cooked, drain it in a colander set in the sink and transfer it to a large serving bowl.

Pour the Zucchini, Almond, and Mint Pesto over the pasta and toss it until the pasta is coated with the pesto.

Lightly drizzle the pasta with the remaining extra virgin olive oil and top it with the slivered almonds.

Serve immediately.

Serves 6

MEASURING CUPS: DRY VERSUS LIQUID

Both kinds of measuring cups actually hold the same amount of dry or liquid ingredients. But dry measuring cups should always be used for ingredients such as flour and sugar so they can be leveled off using a butter knife or the side of a straight frosting spatula.

A liquid measuring cup should be set on the counter when you fill it, but you should then bend down to read the measurements on the side at eye level to be certain it is filled accurately. Liquid measuring cups have spouts to make pouring easier.

Oven-Baked Zucchini Frittata

- 1 tablespoon extra virgin olive oil
- 1 medium onion, thinly sliced
- Salt and pepper to taste
- 2 medium zucchini, thinly sliced (about 4 cups)
- ¼ cup chopped parsley (packed)
- 1 teaspoon extra virgin olive oil for preparing the sauté pan
- 3 teaspoons dried bread crumbs
- 6 eggs
- ⅓ cup grated cheese (Gruyère, Asiago, cheddar, feta, or whatever cheese you like)
- ¼ cup milk
- Paprika

Equipment: cutting board, chef's knife, dry measuring cups, liquid measuring cup, measuring spoons, medium sauté pan, wooden spoon, plate, medium-sized mixing bowl, cheese grater, stand mixer or hand-held mixer or whisk

Preheat the oven to 350 degrees.

Heat 1 tablespoon of extra virgin olive oil in a medium sauté pan over medium-high heat.

Sauté the sliced onions for approximately five minutes, until they begin to soften. Season the onions with a bit of salt and pepper. Add the zucchini and parsley and cook for another 10 minutes. Remove the sauté pan from the heat.

Transfer the onion, zucchini, and parsley mixture onto a plate.

Wash and dry the sauté pan. Brush it with 1 teaspoon of extra virgin olive oil. Sprinkle the bread crumbs on the bottom of the pan.

In a medium-sized mixing bowl, beat the eggs and stir in the cheese and milk.

Arrange the onion, zucchini, and parsley mixture on top of the bread crumbs in the sauté pan. Pour the egg and cheese mixture over the vegetables and sprinkle the top with paprika.

Bake the frittata for approximately 20 minutes, until it is set and browned on top.

Serve immediately.

Serves 4–6

Pure and Simple Oven-Roasted Summer Squashes

- 2 medium-sized zucchini squash
- 2 medium-sized yellow squash
- 3 tablespoons extra virgin olive oil
- 2 teaspoons dried oregano
- Sea salt and pepper to taste

Equipment: cutting board, chef's knife, 2 baking sheets with sides, measuring spoons, pot holders, 2 trivets, spatula, serving platter

Preheat the oven to 375 degrees on the convection setting.

Slice the zucchini and yellow squashes into ¼-inch thick rounds.

Spread out the slices on two baking sheets with sides and sprinkle 1½ tablespoons of the extra virgin olive oil on each pan.

Using clean hands, spread the oil over the squash, coating the slices lightly on both sides.

Sprinkle the dried oregano over the squash.

Roast the squash in the oven for 25–30 minutes or until the slices are browned.

Remove the pans from the oven using pot holders and place them on trivets.

Using a spatula, remove the baked squash rounds from the pans and place them on a serving platter.

Lightly sea salt and pepper to taste.

Serves 4

Chocolate Zucchini Cake

Liquid canola oil to prepare pan
2 tablespoons flour to prepare pan
¾ cup whole-wheat flour (King Arthur White Whole Wheat is nice.)
¾ cup unbleached all-purpose flour
1½ teaspoons baking soda
½ teaspoon sea salt
¾ cup Hershey's Special Dark Cocoa
2 eggs
½ cup organic canola oil
1½ teaspoons pure vanilla extract
½ cup plain nonfat organic yogurt
1 cup packed brown sugar
1 cup boiling water
2 cups zucchini (about 2 small zucchini)

⅓ cup confectioners' sugar

Equipment: mixing bowls, electric mixer, dry measuring cups, liquid measuring cup, measuring spoons, food processor, Bundt pan, wooden spoon, cake tester, butter knife, cake plate

Preheat the oven to 350 degrees.

Brush the inside of the Bundt pan with liquid canola oil, covering the entire inner surface. Sprinkle the 2 tablespoons of flour into the pan and shake it until the whole inside is coated with flour. Turn the pan upside down over the sink and tap it to remove the excess flour.

Measure and combine the flours, baking soda, sea salt, and cocoa in a medium mixing bowl and set it aside.

Using an electric mixer, beat the eggs with the ½ cup of canola oil and vanilla; add the yogurt and beat well.

Add the brown sugar and beat until all ingredients are well combined.

Add the dry ingredients to the egg mixture and mix on medium speed just until all ingredients are blended. The batter will be thick.

Add 1 cup of boiling water and stir with a wooden spoon to combine.

Grate the zucchini in a food processor fitted with a grating blade.

Stir the grated zucchini into the batter with a wooden spoon.

Pour the batter into the prepared Bundt pan.

Hit the bottom of the pan against the countertop two or three times to burst any air bubbles.

Place the cake in the center of the oven and bake it for approximately 30 minutes, until a cake tester comes out clean.

Let the cake cool for at least 30 minutes. Run a butter knife between the edges of the cooled cake and the Bundt pan to loosen the cake. Place a cake plate on top of the Bundt pan and turn them so the pan is upside down. The cake should fall out of the pan onto the plate.

Dust the cake with confectioners' sugar.

Chocolate Zucchini Cake is delicious with slightly sweetened whipped cream.

Serves 12

To vary this recipe slightly, you may add 1 teaspoon ground cinnamon and/or ½ cup chopped walnuts.

Eggplant and Okra

Caramelized Eggplant, Onion, and Tomato Pizza with Fresh Basil

- 4 small eggplants (each the size of a baseball)
- 2 teaspoons sea salt
- Water
- 1 sweet onion
- 4 plum tomatoes
- 2 cloves garlic
- 1 scant teaspoon sugar
- ¼ cup extra virgin olive oil
- 1 teaspoon sea salt
- 1 partially baked Whole-Wheat Pizza Crust (recipe on page 132)
- ⅓ cup grated Parmesan or Asiago cheese
- ⅓ cup chopped fresh basil leaves

Equipment: cutting board, chef's knife, large bowl, plate, colander, large sauté pan, measuring spoons, liquid measuring cup, dry measuring cups, wooden spoon, pizza stone, pizza cutter

Wash the eggplants and dice them into bite-sized pieces.

Place the diced eggplant in a large bowl of water to which you've added the 2 teaspoons of sea salt. Put a plate on top of the eggplant to keep it submerged and soak it for 15 minutes.

While the eggplant soaks, dice the onion and tomatoes.

Smash the cloves of garlic with the handle of a chef's knife, remove their peels, and then chop them.

Drain the eggplant in the colander. Run water over the eggplant to rinse it and then shake off excess water.

Heat the extra virgin olive oil in a large sauté pan over medium-high heat. Put the eggplant, onion, tomatoes, garlic, sugar, and 1 teaspoon of sea salt into the pan and stir them together with a wooden spoon.

Cover the pan, lower the heat to medium, and cook for approximately 30 minutes.

Remove the lid from the pan and cook uncovered until all the liquid has evaporated, about 10 minutes longer, until the vegetables are caramelized.

When the vegetables are done, remove the pan from the heat. The vegetables should be very soft.

Spread the caramelized eggplant, tomatoes, and onion evenly over the partially baked pizza crust and top it with the grated cheese.

Bake the pizza for 8 minutes, until the crust is thoroughly baked and the topping is bubbly.

Carefully remove the pizza from the oven and sprinkle it with chopped basil leaves.

Let the pizza sit for 5 minutes, then cut it into wedges and serve.

Serves 4–6

Katie's Classic Eggplant Parmesan

3 Ichiban Japanese eggplants
½ cup unbleached all-purpose flour
Sea salt
¼ teaspoon black pepper
2 eggs
⅓ cup nonfat milk
1½ cups dried bread crumbs
2 cloves garlic, minced
½ cup finely chopped parsley
½ cup extra virgin olive oil
2 tablespoons Parmesan cheese

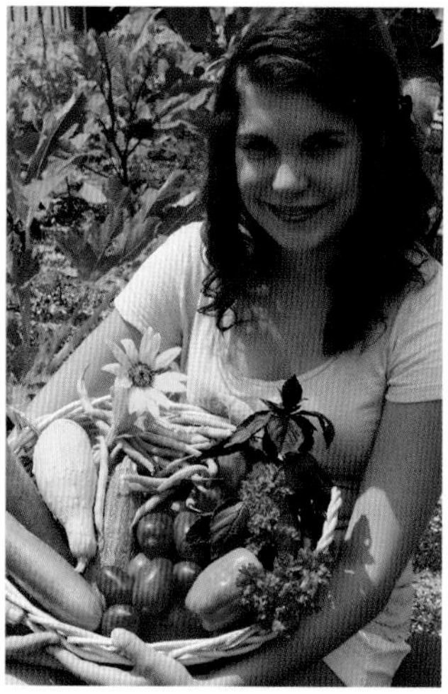
Katie Stagliano

Katie Stagliano started growing vegetables in third grade, when her cabbage seedling grew into a forty-pound cabbage. Concerned about the needs of the hungry in her community, she took the giant cabbage to a local soup kitchen. She then convinced her school's headmaster to allow her and a group of her friends to start a vegetable garden on campus so they could grow food to feed the hungry. Today she heads her own nonprofit organization, Katie's Krops (read her story online at www.katieskrops.com). The following recipe is based on one of Katie's favorites.

Equipment: cutting board, paring knife, chef's knife, colander, measuring spoons, dry measuring cups, liquid measuring cup, 3 shallow bowls, clean kitchen towel, large sauté pan, plate covered with paper towels, serving platter

Cut the eggplant into ¼-inch slices. Lightly salt the slices and put them aside in a colander set in the sink to drain.

Prepare the three shallow bowls as follows:

First bowl: combine the flour, ½ teaspoon sea salt, and ¼ teaspoon black pepper.

Second bowl: stir together the eggs and milk.

Third bowl: combine the bread crumbs, minced garlic, and finely chopped parsley.

Dry each slice of eggplant with a clean kitchen towel.

Dip a slice of eggplant in the first bowl and coat it well with the flour mixture; move the slice to the second bowl and coat it well with the egg-and-milk mixture; move the slice to the third bowl and coat it fully with bread crumbs. Repeat this procedure with each slice of eggplant.

Heat the extra virgin olive oil in a large sauté pan over medium-high heat. Add several coated eggplant slices and cook them about 3 minutes per side (or until golden brown). Remove the browned eggplant to a plate covered with paper towels. Continue cooking slices of eggplant until all are browned. If the oil begins to smoke, lower the heat a bit.

Dust the warm eggplant with shredded Parmesan cheese.

Katie's Classic Eggplant Parmesan is delicious served with Chunky Savory Tomato Sauce (page 53) or with Yogurt Ranch Dressing (page 112).

Serves 4 as a dinner entrée or 6 as an appetizer

Oven-Roasted Okra Fries with Dried Herbs

- 3 cups okra
- 1 tablespoon extra virgin olive oil
- 2 tablespoons dried herbes de Provence

Equipment: dry measuring cups, measuring spoons, colander, cutting board, chef's knife, baking sheet with sides, pot holders, trivets

Preheat the oven to 400 degrees on the convection setting.

Wash and trim the okra, cutting the stems close to the pods while being careful not to pierce the pods.

Spread the okra in a single layer on a large baking sheet with sides, leaving space between the pods.

Pour extra virgin olive oil over the okra and toss it with clean hands to coat the okra thoroughly.

Sprinkle the dried herbs over the okra.

Place the pan in the middle of the preheated oven and roast the okra for 20 minutes or until the pods are crispy and brown on all sides. If you roast the okra on a conventional oven setting, then turn the pods with a spatula halfway through the cooking time so they will brown all over.

Serve immediately, either plain or with Yogurt Ranch Dressing (page 112).

Garlic

Garlicky, Lemony Hummus

- 1 15-ounce can of chickpeas, drained and rinsed
- 3 medium garlic cloves, peeled
- ½ teaspoon sea salt
- Pinch of cayenne pepper
- Juice of 1 large lemon
- ¼ cup tahini (sesame paste)
- ¼ cup extra virgin olive oil
- ¼ cup water

You can serve hummus as a sandwich spread on crusty whole-grain bread with sprouts, lettuce, and tomato. It is also delicious eaten with crudités (raw, cut-up vegetables such as carrots, celery, broccoli, and peppers).

Equipment: can opener, garlic press, lemon squeezer or juicer, dry measuring cups, liquid measuring cup, measuring spoons, food processor, serving bowl

Place all the ingredients in a food processor fitted with a steel blade and process until the mixture is smooth and well blended (about 45 seconds).

Transfer the hummus to a bowl, cover it, and store it in the refrigerator. Make the recipe about 30 minutes before you want to serve it so all the flavors have time to blend.

Makes about 2 cups and serves 6–8

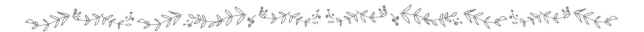

GARLIC

Garlic is one of the main flavors used in TMD cooking. You'll notice we use freshly minced garlic in most recipes.

Garlic is in the onion family, and the bulb, which grows underground, is made up of many (about 10–20) sections, called *cloves*. Each clove is wrapped in its own paperlike skin, which is not eaten. It can be a pain to peel the cloves, but there is truly no substitute for the taste of freshly minced garlic—not to mention the many health benefits it imparts, such as helping to prevent heart disease, high cholesterol, high blood pressure, and even the common cold! So here are some steps to easy peeling:

- Separate cloves from the bulb by inserting a paring knife between two cloves and wiggling it to pry them from the stalk at the center of the bulb.
- Take off as many cloves as you need.
- Place the heavy handle of a chef's knife on top of one clove and press down hard on it with one hand on top of the other to smash the garlic. This will tear and loosen the peel, which will then come off easily.
- You can now mince or slice the garlic clove with your knife or use a garlic press to do the job of fine mincing.

I prefer the press because it makes the garlic very fine. My garlic press also has a slicer option, which I use for recipes such as Cherry Tomato and Garlic-Bread Bake (page 78), which calls for a lot of garlic.

Note (see photo below): There is a cute little "gizmo" or gadget for peeling garlic that really works well. It looks like a manicotti or cannoli shell, but it's made of a pliable silicone rubber. You can place several cloves in it at once and roll it on the counter. The skin comes off the cloves easily.

Sautéed Greens with Garlic over Pasta

- A large colander filled with greens of your choice
- 6 cloves of garlic, peeled
- 2 tablespoons extra virgin olive oil
- ¼ teaspoon red-pepper flakes
- 1 pound penne pasta
- Shredded Asiago cheese to garnish

Equipment: colander, salad spinner, cutting board, chef's knife, garlic press, large sauté pan, measuring spoons, pasta pot, pot holders, wooden spoon

Soak and rinse the greens (as described on page 40).

Chop the greens into bite-sized pieces and spin them in the salad spinner to dry them.

Mince the garlic.

Heat the extra virgin olive oil in a large sauté pan over medium-high heat. Lightly brown the minced garlic in the oil, being careful not to burn it. Stir it occasionally with a wooden spoon.

Add the greens to the pan and stir them until they are blended with the oil and garlic. Cook them until they are tender and wilted, add the red-pepper flakes, and remove the pan from the heat.

Cook the pasta according to package directions. When it is done, carefully drain it in the colander, pouring the pan contents away from you to avoid the steam.

Pour the cooked pasta from the colander into the pan of greens. Toss to combine and then reheat.

Garnish the greens and pasta with Asiago cheese.

Serve immediately.

Serves 6

CHOOSING GREENS

This recipe would work well with any of the following homegrown greens (or a combination): kale, swiss chard, mustard greens, spinach, broccoli rabe.

Cherry Tomato and Garlic-Bread Bake

- 1 loaf crusty whole-grain bread, sliced ½ inch thick
- 4 tablespoons extra virgin olive oil, and a bit more for preparing the casserole dish
- 1 clove of garlic, peeled and halved
- 2 medium-sized yellow onions
- 1 medium-sized head of garlic
- 4 cups cherry, grape, pink, or yellow-pear tomatoes, whole
- ¾ cup coarsely chopped sweet basil leaves
- 4 ounces Parmesan, Romano, or Asiago cheese, shredded
- 3 cups of DIY Vegetable Stock (recipe on page 136)
- Sea salt and black pepper to taste
- Whole basil leaves for garnish

Equipment: dry measuring cups, liquid measuring cups, baking sheet with sides, basting brush, silicone-rubber garlic peeler, garlic press, large sauté pan, bread knife, paring knife, cutting board, ladle, oven-proof casserole dish, medium-sized pot

Preheat the broiler.

Toast the slices of bread on baking sheets under the broiler until they are golden brown, turning them once so that the two sides toast evenly.

Remove the toast from the broiler, brush both sides of the slices with extra virgin olive oil (2 tablespoons total), and rub one side of each piece with the cut side of the halved garlic clove.

Preheat the oven to 375 degrees.

Slice the onions. Heat the remaining 2 tablespoons of the extra virgin olive oil in a large sauté pan and cook the onions over medium heat, stirring occasionally until they are soft and light brown, about 15 minutes.

While the onions are cooking, separate the garlic cloves and, using a silicone-rubber garlic peeler, remove the skins. Slice all the cloves using a garlic press.

When the onions are light brown, add the sliced garlic to the sauté pan and cook for another 3 minutes. Remove the pan from the heat and set it aside.

Brush the bottom and sides of an 8×10-inch ovenproof casserole dish with extra virgin olive oil.

Place half the toast on the bottom of the pan and cover it with half the sautéed onion and sliced garlic. Top the onion and garlic with half the tomatoes and all the chopped basil.

Sprinkle a third of the cheese on top of the tomatoes and basil.

Repeat the process, layering the rest of the toast, the onions and garlic, the tomatoes, and half of the remaining cheese.

Season the vegetable stock with sea salt and black pepper to taste and pour it over the bread mixture, wait a few minutes until the stock is absorbed, and top the mixture with the remaining shredded cheese.

Cover the dish with aluminum foil and bake for 35 minutes. Remove the foil, turn up the temperature to 400 degrees, and bake until the top is golden brown (approximately 15–20 minutes).

Remove the dish from the oven and cool it a bit before cutting it into 8 pieces.

Garnish the dish with the whole basil leaves.

Serves 8

Beans

Butter Beans with Fresh Mint

2 cups fresh, shelled butter beans

2 teaspoons extra virgin olive oil

½ cup fresh mint leaves, finely chopped (no stems)

Sea salt and pepper to taste

Equipment: dry measuring cups, measuring spoons, medium-sized saucepan, colander, large bowl, cutting board, chef's knife, medium-sized sauté pan, wooden spoon, serving bowl

Half fill a medium-sized saucepan with water, cover the pan, and bring the water to a boil over high heat.

Fill a large bowl with ice and cold water.

Drop the butter beans into the boiling water and, after the water returns to a boil, cook the beans for 3–4 minutes to blanch them. Remove the beans from the heat and drain them using a colander.

Transfer the beans into the large bowl filled with ice water. Then drain the beans in the colander again.

In a medium sauté pan over medium-high heat, warm the extra virgin olive oil and add the butter beans. Toss them gently in the pan to coat with oil.

Add ½ cup of water and cook the beans uncovered until the water has evaporated (approximately 7 minutes).

Transfer the beans to a serving bowl. Sprinkle them with the finely chopped mint leaves and toss to combine. Taste the beans and season them with a bit of sea salt and freshly ground black pepper.

Serve immediately.

Serves 6

A large bowl of green beans (about 1 pound)

3 tablespoons extra virgin olive oil

3 cloves garlic, thinly sliced

3-inch piece of fresh ginger, peeled and julienned

1 teaspoon sea salt

½ cup dry white wine or water

⅓ cup slivered almonds for garnish

Sautéed green beans with ginger are delicious served over steamed brown rice.

Sautéed Green Beans with Ginger

Equipment: colander, cutting board, chef's knife, garlic press, paring knife, measuring spoons, liquid measuring cup, dry measuring cups, large sauté pan with cover, wooden spoon, serving bowl

Put the beans in a colander and rinse them. Trim off their stems.

Heat the extra virgin olive oil in a large sauté pan over medium-high heat.

Sauté the garlic and ginger in the oil for a few minutes until the garlic begins to brown.

Add the green beans to the pan. Sprinkle them with sea salt and stir them with a wooden spoon to distribute the salt.

Pour the wine or water over the beans, cover the pan, reduce the heat to medium, and cook for 5 minutes.

Remove the cover from the pan, reduce the heat to low, and simmer the beans until the liquid has nearly evaporated (about 3 minutes).

Transfer the green beans to a serving bowl, garnish with slivered almonds, and serve immediately.

Serves 6

Green Beans with Mustard Sauce

Equipment: colander, cutting board, chef's knife, large sauté pan with lid, wooden spoon, garlic press, liquid measuring cup, dry measuring cup, measuring spoons, serving bowl or platter

A large bowl of green beans (about 1 pound)

3 tablespoons extra virgin olive oil

3 cloves garlic, minced

½ cup dry white wine or apple juice

1 tablespoon Dijon mustard

⅓ cup toasted slivered almonds for garnish

Put the beans in a colander and rinse them. Trim off their stems.

Heat the extra virgin olive oil in a large sauté pan over medium-high heat.

Add the minced garlic and cook it until it just begins to brown.

Add the green beans and stir them until they are coated with the oil.

Add the wine or juice and reduce the heat to simmer.

Cover the pan and cook the beans until they are tender (about 5 minutes).

Uncover the pan and toss the beans with the Dijon mustard. Stir the beans over the heat for about 3 minutes.

Remove the beans from the heat, transfer them to a serving dish, and top them with the slivered almonds.

Serve immediately.

Serves 6

Greens

Broccoli Rabe and Garlic Pizza

- 1 large bunch of broccoli rabe (about 4–5 cups chopped)
- 3 tablespoons extra virgin olive oil
- 5–6 cloves garlic, peeled and minced
- ¼ teaspoon red-pepper flakes
- Sea salt and pepper to taste
- 1 recipe Chunky Savory Tomato Sauce (recipe on page 53)
- 1 partially baked Whole-Wheat Pizza Crust (recipe on page 132)
- ½ cup shredded Asiago cheese

Equipment: pizza stone, cutting board, chef's knife, salad spinner, garlic mincer, measuring spoons, dry measuring cups, wooden spoon, large sauté pan, pot holders, 2 trivets, pizza cutter

Place the pizza stone in the oven and preheat it to 500 degrees.

Wash and cut up the broccoli rabe, discarding the thickest parts of the stems. I use the stems only where the leaves begin. Use a salad spinner to wash and dry the greens.

Heat the extra virgin olive oil over medium-high heat in a large sauté pan.

Sauté the garlic in the oil until it begins to brown.

Add the broccoli rabe and red-pepper flakes and cook for 5 minutes until the greens are tender and partially wilted.

Add a light sprinkle of sea salt and pepper and remove the pan from the heat.

Top the partially baked pizza crust with the Chunky Savory Tomato Sauce and the sautéed broccoli rabe.

If you use arugula or spinach, use tongs or a fork to place it on the pizza so you don't add extra moisture from the sauté pan.

Top the greens with the Asiago cheese.

Bake the pizza on the pizza stone until it is fully cooked, with its bottom browned and the sauce bubbling hot (about 8 minutes).

Using pot holders, carefully remove the pizza with the pizza stone from the oven and slide the pizza onto a large cutting board.

Place the pizza stone on trivets to cool.

Let the pizza sit for a few minutes before slicing it with the pizza cutter.

Serves 4–6

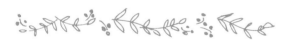

Oven-Baked Kale Chips with Sesame Seeds

- 24 tender kale leaves
- 2 tablespoons extra virgin olive oil
- 2 teaspoons whole sesame seeds
- 2 sprinkles of sea salt

Equipment: cutting board, chef's knife, salad spinner, clean kitchen towel, large bowl, measuring spoons, 2–3 baking sheets with sides, metal spatula, pot holders, serving bowl

Preheat the oven to 375 degrees on the convection setting.

Wash the kale leaves, removing and discarding the center stems.

Tear the leaves into pieces about two inches by two inches.

Dry the kale in a salad spinner and then blot it with a clean kitchen towel to remove excess water.

Put the kale pieces in a large bowl and pour the extra virgin olive oil over them. Using clean hands, rub the oil onto the kale pieces to coat them thoroughly.

Spread the kale pieces in a single layer on the baking sheets with sides, making sure they do not overlap.

Sprinkle the kale lightly with sesame seeds.

Place the sheets on racks positioned in the center of the oven.

Set your timer for 6 minutes and check the kale at that stage. With a single layer of chips they should be done, but they may need to cook another minute. The kale chips should look dark green and dry. If the kale turns brown, it becomes bitter.

Remove the baking sheets from the oven and slide the chips into a bowl using a metal spatula. Lightly sprinkle them with sea salt and eat immediately. Yum!

Serves 4 (but I can easily eat all these myself!)

Some types of kale leaves are denser than others. I used Dwarf Siberian Kale in this recipe. Dinosaur Kale is thicker and may need to bake longer. Test a few kale pieces first to determine your desired cooking time. And don't salt the chips until they are done. Salting before cooking draws the water out of the leaves and slows the crisping process.

Spinach, Feta, and Dill Pies

- 6 cups fresh baby spinach leaves (about 10 ounces)
- 8 ounces sheep's milk feta cheese
- ⅓ cup finely chopped fresh dill
- 1 egg
- Sea salt and pepper to taste
- ¼ cup butter (4 tablespoons)
- ¼ cup extra virgin olive oil
- ½ pound prepared frozen filo dough thawed in the refrigerator for 24 hours before using

Equipment: cutting board, chef's knife, salad spinner, large bowl, small bowl, small wire whisk or fork, large wooden spoon, liquid measuring cup, small sauté pan, measuring spoons, basting brush, 2–3 baking sheets with sides

Preheat the oven to 375 degrees.

Wash and spin the spinach leaves. Feel free to use the stems if they are small and thin.

Roughly chop the spinach and place it in the large bowl.

Add the finely chopped dill to the bowl as well.

Lightly beat the egg in the small bowl and pour it into the spinach and dill.

Using clean hands, blend the contents of the bowl so the egg coats the spinach and dill.

Crumble in the feta cheese.

Lightly sprinkle the mixture with sea salt and black pepper.

Blend all ingredients together with a large wooden spoon and set aside the bowl.

Melt the butter in the sauté pan and, when it is liquid, add the extra virgin olive oil and stir with the brush.

Remove the outer wrapper from the roll of filo dough. Cut the roll into thirds. Place two-thirds of the dough back in the refrigerator.

Unroll the remaining filo in front of you on a clean surface and brush the top layer with the butter and olive-oil mixture.

Place a tablespoon of spinach filling at the end closest to you and begin to fold the dough as you would an American flag or a paper football in school:

- Lift the top two sheets of filo from the lower left-hand corner and bring them across to meet the right edge of the filo.
- Fold the dough straight upward and then across to the left edge. Continue folding up and right, then up and left to create an isosceles triangle.
- Continue folding up and right, then up and left to create an isosceles triangle.

When the packet is complete, brush the entire exterior with the butter and extra virgin olive oil mixture and place it on a baking sheet.

Brush each new top layer of filo with the butter and olive-oil mixture before placing 1 tablespoon of spinach filling at the end closest to you.

Continue to fold the pies as described above. Place them all on the baking sheets, leaving enough room between them so they do not touch.

When the baking sheets are filled, place them in the oven and bake the pies for approximately 25–30 minutes or until they are golden brown.

Makes 30 pieces

Kale Soup with Butter Beans

- 1 cup shelled butter beans, rinsed
- 15 leaves of kale (any variety)
- 3 tablespoons extra virgin olive oil
- 1 medium onion, diced finely
- 3 cloves garlic, minced
- 6 cups DIY Vegetable Stock (recipe on page 136)
- 1 loaf thick-cut crusty bread, toasted and drizzled with extra virgin olive oil
- Sea salt
- Freshly ground black pepper

Equipment: dry measuring cups, colander, liquid measuring cup, measuring spoons, cutting board, chef's knife, garlic press, salad spinner, medium-sized saucepan, stockpot

Blanch the fresh butter beans by dropping them into a medium-sized saucepan of boiling water and cooking them for 3–4 minutes. Turn off the heat and drain the beans in a colander.

Cut off the thick stems of the kale and discard them in your kitchen compost bucket. Chop the kale into approximately one-inch pieces.

Pour the extra virgin olive oil into the stockpot and heat it over medium-high heat. Add the diced onion, lower the heat to medium, and sauté the onion slowly, with the pot uncovered, until it is soft and translucent, approximately 10 minutes.

Add the minced garlic and sauté it for a few minutes until it begins to brown.

Add the chopped kale and stir to combine the ingredients.

Ladle 6 cups of vegetable stock over the kale. Turn up the heat, cover the pot, and bring the mixture to a boil.

Add the butter beans and stir the soup to distribute them evenly.

Lower the heat and simmer for approximately 30 minutes or until the kale is soft and the butter beans are tender.

Taste the soup and season it with salt and pepper.

Serve the soup with crusty toast drizzled with extra virgin olive oil.

Serves 4–6

Cabbage

Cabbage, Walnut, and Cranberry Salad

½ medium cabbage, cored and shredded (6 cups)
1 cup chopped walnuts
1 cup dried cranberries

Dressing:
¼ cup extra virgin olive oil
2 tablespoons balsamic vinegar
2 cloves garlic, minced
1½ teaspoons dried oregano
Sea salt and freshly ground black pepper to taste
Several sprigs of fresh oregano for garnish

Equipment: large pot for cleaning the cabbage, cutting board, chef's knife, large bowl, garlic press, dry measuring cups, liquid measuring cups, measuring spoons, serving bowl

Cut the cabbage in half and remove the core and outer leaves. Deposit the core and outer leaves in your kitchen compost bucket. Soak the cabbage halves in a pot of warm water for a few minutes to draw out any flecks of dirt or "critters."

Rinse the cabbage and store half the head in the refrigerator for future use. Slice the remaining cabbage into long, thin strips.

In a large mixing bowl, combine the shredded cabbage, chopped walnuts, and dried cranberries.

Make the dressing by whisking together the extra virgin olive oil, balsamic vinegar, minced garlic, dried oregano, salt, and pepper.

Pour the dressing over the cabbage, walnuts, and cranberries and toss the salad until all the cabbage is coated with the dressing.

Spoon the salad into individual salad bowls and top with leaves of the fresh oregano pulled from the stems.

Serves 6

Stop and taste the cabbage. Its sweet, clean taste is extremely satisfying. You might like to keep a bag of clean shredded cabbage in your refrigerator to use as a crunchy snack or to add to a salad.

Roasted Potatoes, Red Onion, and Cabbage

1 medium cabbage

1½ pounds small red potatoes (about 15)

1 large red onion

2 teaspoons caraway seeds

6 tablespoons extra virgin olive oil

2 cups DIY Vegetable Stock (recipe on page 136)

⅓ cup chopped parsley

Sea salt

Equipment: large pot for cleaning cabbage, cutting board, chef's knife, measuring spoons, liquid measuring cup, dry measuring cup, large shallow baking dish, pot holders

Preheat the oven to 400 degrees on the convection setting.

Discard the outer leaves of the head of cabbage. Cut the cabbage in half and soak it in a large pot of warm water for a few minutes to draw out any flecks of dirt or "critters."

Remove the cabbage from the water and cut it into about eight small wedges, leaving the core, which will hold each piece together.

Wash the baby red potatoes and cut them in half.

Peel the red onion and dice it into large pieces.

Place all the veggies and the caraway seeds in a shallow baking pan and toss them with the extra virgin olive oil.

Pour the vegetable stock over the vegetables and bake them for about 1 hour, until the vegetables are tender and the cabbage and potatoes have browned a bit.

Season the vegetables with sea salt and top them with chopped parsley before serving.

Serves 8

Arugula-Stuffed Fish Fillets with Fennel and Lemon

- 4 fillets of branzino or red snapper
- 4 cups arugula
- Sea salt
- Black pepper
- 1 bulb fennel
- 2 small lemons
- 1 cup white wine
- 4 tablespoons extra virgin olive oil
- 2 lemons for juice
- ⅔ cup fresh parsley leaves, finely chopped

Equipment: grill or broiler, aluminum foil, chef's knife, cutting board, measuring spoons, liquid measuring cup, dry measuring cups

Heat the grill or broiler to high.

Rinse and dry each fish fillet. Cut four pieces of aluminum foil large enough to fold into a packet with room for air.

Wash, stem, and roughly chop the arugula.

Place a quarter of the arugula on each piece of foil and lay the fish fillets on top of the arugula.

Season the fish with sea salt and pepper.

Wash the fennel bulb and cut it in half. Remove the dense core and put it in your kitchen compost bucket. Slice the remaining parts of the bulb into long strips.

Cut the lemons into round slices.

Top the fish with the fennel and lemon slices.

Turn up the edges of each piece of foil to form a small bowl or canoe shape. Pour ¼ cup of the white wine and then 1 tablespoon of the extra virgin olive oil over each fillet.

Fold the aluminum-foil packets well, leaving a pocket of air.

Place the packets on a hot grill or under the broiler and cook them for 20 minutes.

Carefully remove the packets from the grill or broiler, open them, and transfer the contents to individual serving plates.

Squeeze lemon juice over the fish and top it with chopped fresh parsley. Serve with grilled vegetables.

Serves 4

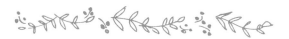

Radicchio and Fennel Salad with Shrimp, Avocado, Fresh Parsley, and Lime

1 bulb fennel

1 head radicchio

Vinaigrette:

3 tablespoons extra virgin olive oil

1 tablespoon red wine vinegar

¼ teaspoon sea salt and several grinds of black pepper

1 tablespoon extra virgin olive oil

1 pound shrimp, peeled and deveined

Juice of one lime

¼ cup finely chopped parsley

1 avocado

Equipment: cutting board, chef's knife, shrimp zipper or paring knife, measuring spoons, small bowl, whisk, dry measuring cups, medium-sized bowl, medium-sized sauté pan, slotted spoon, large serving platter

HOW TO PEEL AND DEVEIN SHRIMP

If you buy local shrimp, you may find that it comes complete with the heads still attached. If so, with each shrimp remove the head first by snapping it back and pulling it off. Next pull off the legs.

The easiest method I know to peel and devein shrimp is to use a "shrimp zipper," a device that removes the shell and dark vein that runs along the shrimp's back. Slide the zipper under the shell at the head end of the shrimp and gently rock the zipper slightly up and down, moving it along the shrimp's back toward the tail. As you rock the zipper, the shell will split and come off and the dark vein will be removed.

If you don't own a shrimp zipper, you can peel off the shell by hand and then use a small paring knife to remove the vein, which runs just under the surface of the flesh. First slice the flesh along the top of the vein and then remove the vein with the point of the knife. The vein is sticky, so keep a paper towel on the counter to wipe the blade clean after you devein each shrimp.

Wash the fennel bulb and cut it in half. Remove the dense core and put it in your kitchen compost bucket. Wash the head of radicchio and cut it in half.

Thinly slice the fennel and radicchio and toss them together in a large serving bowl.

Whisk together the ingredients for the vinaigrette—extra virgin olive oil, vinegar, and a sprinkle of sea salt and pepper—in a small bowl and set aside.

Dress the radicchio and fennel with the vinaigrette and toss to coat well.

Heat 1 tablespoon of extra virgin olive oil in a medium-sized sauté pan over medium-high heat and cook the shrimp until it turns pink and opaque.

Remove the shrimp from the pan, put it in a medium-sized bowl, and squeeze the lime juice over it. Then add the finely chopped parsley and toss to coat the shrimp.

Place the fennel and radicchio on a large serving platter.

Arrange the shrimp on top of the salad.

Peel the avocado with a paring knife. Carefully cut it in half lengthwise (the flesh can be slippery). A regular flatware teaspoon can be used to remove the pit. Cut the avocado into thin wedges and arrange them on the salad.

Serve immediately.

Serves 6–8

GRILLED GARDEN VEGGIES

Wash your choice of garden veggies—such as eggplant, zucchini, other summer squashes, and bell peppers—and slice them into uniform sizes. Brush them with a little extra virgin olive oil. Place them on a clean medium-hot grill and cook for 3–4 minutes. Turn them once and grill the other side for another 3–4 minutes. (Cooking times will vary somewhat depending on the density of the vegetables, so keep a close eye on them.)

Most grilled veggies taste better than their steamed counterparts because the grill caramelizes the vegetables by drawing water from them. The extra virgin olive oil adds to the flavor and helps prevent sticking.

Try finely chopped herbs on your grilled vegetables for a real treat.

Winter Squashes

Oven-Roasted Winter Squashes

Equipment: cutting board, chef's knife, tablespoon, colander, 2 clean kitchen towels, measuring spoons, baking sheet with sides, microplane grater, pot holders, trivet, medium-sized bowl, spatula

- 2 small winter squashes (butternut, acorn, tiny pumpkins, or other winter squashes)
- 3 tablespoons extra virgin olive oil (or 2 tablespoons if the squashes are very small, like the ones in the picture)
- 1 dried nutmeg seed
- 1 teaspoon cinnamon
- 1 tablespoon real maple syrup or local honey

For toasting squash seeds:

- Seeds from 2 winter squashes
- 1 tablespoon extra virgin olive oil
- Sprinklings of spices of your choice (such as nutmeg, ginger, cinnamon, cayenne pepper, sea salt, or pepper)

Preheat the oven to 375 degrees.

Wash the skin of the squashes.

Using a heavy knife, slice each squash in half. Scoop out the seeds.

Put the seeds in a colander and wash them, then remove their pulp. Place the seeds in a bowl of warm water to soak.

Place the squash halves cut side up on a baking sheet with sides. Drizzle each piece with a quarter of the extra virgin olive oil.

Grate the nutmeg seed over the squash, using 3–4 gratings on each piece.

Sprinkle a quarter of the cinnamon over each piece of squash.

Lightly drizzle a quarter of the maple syrup or honey over each piece of squash.

Bake the squash for 45 minutes, until it is very soft. (The tiny ones in the picture took only 30 minutes.)

While the squash is baking decide which of your favorite spices to use for coating the squash seeds. You may use nutmeg, cinnamon, and ginger—or a bit of sea salt, pepper, and a light sprinkle of cayenne pepper if you like things hot. (If you use cayenne, start with only a small sprinkle. Cayenne is extremely hot.)

Drain the water from the seeds using a colander in the sink. Set the seeds in a single layer on a clean kitchen towel to dry. Pat them with another towel to remove excess water.

Place the seeds in a single layer on a baking sheet with sides. To dry the seeds place the pan in the oven with the squash for 4 minutes.

Using pot holders, remove the tray of seeds and place it on a trivet.

When the pan has cooled a bit, use a spatula to scrape the seeds into a medium-sized bowl. Pour 1 teaspoon of extra virgin olive oil over the seeds. Using clean hands, toss the seeds until all are coated with the oil.

Spread the seeds on the pan again, making sure they are in one layer. Sprinkle the seeds with the seasonings of your choice.

When 5 minutes remain on the cooking time for the squash, put the seeds in the oven and let them toast until they have browned a bit (but do not burn). Remove the seeds when they are browned.

When the squash is tender, carefully remove the pan from the oven using pot holders and place it on a trivet.

Transfer the squash halves to a serving platter, or to individual plates, and top them with the toasted, seasoned seeds.

Serve immediately.

Serves 4

Curried Butternut-Squash and Apple Soup

Equipment: large stockpot, wooden spoon, cutting board, chef's knife, paring knife, vegetable peeler, food processor, liquid measuring cup, slotted spoon, ladle, measuring spoons

4 tablespoons extra virgin olive oil

1 large onion, finely chopped (about 2 cups)

4 teaspoons curry powder

2 medium-sized butternut squashes (about 3 pounds)

2 apples, peeled, cored, and chopped

4 cups DIY Vegetable Stock (recipe on page 136)

1 cup apple juice

Heat the extra virgin olive oil in a large stockpot over medium-high heat and sauté the finely chopped onion until soft, about 10 minutes. If the onion starts to brown, lower the heat. It should be soft and translucent. Add the curry powder and stir well.

While the onion is cooking, peel and cut up the butternut squashes (see sidebar on page 104).

Reserve the seeds and toast them according to the directions on page 102.

Add the chunks of butternut squash, the cut-up apples, and the DIY Vegetable Stock to the stockpot.

Bring the soup to a boil, lower the heat to simmer, and cook it partially covered until the squash is very tender, about 25 minutes. Turn off the heat.

Using a slotted spoon, move the solids from the soup to a food processor fitted with a steel blade, ladle in one cup of the cooking liquid ("stock"), and pulse the mixture until it is well pureed. Add additional stock if needed to achieve the desired consistency. (If you plan to wait a day or two before serving this soup, reserve about 1 cup of the stock to thin the soup when you reheat it.)

Return the puree to the stockpot, add the apple juice, reheat the soup, and stir to combine well.

Serve immediately, garnishing each serving with some toasted squash seeds.

Serves 6–8

PEELING AND CUTTING WINTER SQUASHES

Dealing with winter squashes and pumpkins can be difficult because they tend to be dense and hard. Cut off both ends first. If the kind of squash you're using has a longer "neck," cut it from the rounder bottom. If you have a sharp vegetable peeler, you can use it to peel the skin off the neck. Butternut squash has a rather slimy juice, which may make your hands slide, so have a hand towel nearby. If your peeler is not up to the task, try a paring knife. When you get to the round bottom, cut it in half using a heavy chef's knife and scoop out the seeds with a tablespoon. Then you can peel the bottom pieces, using whichever implement worked best on the neck.

Butternut-Squash and Apple Soup with Autumn Spices

Equipment: large stockpot, cutting board, chef's knife, measuring spoons, liquid measuring cup, paring knife, vegetable peeler, food processor, large slotted spoon, ladle

- 3 tablespoons extra virgin olive oil
- 1 large onion, diced
- ½ teaspoon ground nutmeg
- ¼ teaspoon ground ginger
- ¼ teaspoon ground cloves
- 1 teaspoon ground cinnamon
- 2 pounds of butternut squash (I medium or 2 small), peeled and cubed into large chunks
- 2 apples, peeled, cored, and roughly chopped
- 4 cups DIY Vegetable Stock (recipe on page 136)
- 1 cup apple juice
- Sea salt and freshly ground black pepper to taste
- 1 extra apple for garnish

Heat the extra virgin olive oil in a large stockpot and sauté the onion, stirring occasionally, for about 10 minutes over medium-high heat until it is soft.

Add the spices and cook for a few minutes to blend the flavors.

Add the butternut squash, apples, and DIY Vegetable Stock.

Cover the pot, turn up the heat, and bring the soup to a boil.

Reduce the heat and simmer the soup partially covered for about 25 minutes or until the squash is tender.

Turn off the heat.

With a slotted spoon transfer the solids to a food processor fitted with a steel blade.

Ladle 1 cup of stock into the processor bowl and puree the mixture until it is smooth. Add more stock until the soup is the desired consistency.

Save any remaining stock.

Return the puree to the stockpot, add the apple juice, and reheat the soup until it's very hot.

Season it with a bit of sea salt and a few good grinds of fresh black pepper.

Ladle the soup into bowls and garnish it with thin slices of apple.

You can make the soup a day or two before serving it. When you reheat it, the soup will naturally thicken as it cooks, so you may need to thin it by adding extra stock. The same applies to leftover soup. Use the extra stock from this recipe to thin it to the desired consistency.

Serves 6–8

Peppers

Roasted Red-Pepper Hummus

Equipment: broiler pan, long handled fork, can opener, colander, garlic mincer, lemon squeezer or juicer, measuring spoons, liquid measuring cup, paper bag, food processor, cutting board, paring knife, serving bowl, trivet

- 2 large red bell peppers, roasted
- 1 clove of garlic, peeled
- 1 15-ounce can of chickpeas, drained and rinsed
- Juice of ½ lemon
- ¼ cup extra virgin olive oil
- 1 small sprinkle of cayenne pepper

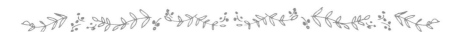

Preheat the broiler. Wash the whole peppers and place them on a broiler pan.

Broil the peppers, turning them with a large fork until they are charred (blackened) on all sides.

When the peppers are completely charred, remove the broiler pan from the broiler, place it on a trivet, and turn off the heat.

BELL PEPPERS

Red, green, and yellow bell peppers are fun to grow and a great source of vitamin C.

Their crunch makes them a great snack plain or with a dip such as Yogurt Ranch Dressing (page 112) or Garlicky, Lemony Hummus (page 74).

They also liven up a garden salad with flavor, color, and texture.

Try roasting them (see directions in Roasted Red-Pepper Hummus) and topping your favorite sandwich. With their soft sweetness, they're great with any kind of cheese, tuna, or meat. They also go well with roasted-vegetable or avocado sandwiches.

They may not be so wonderful with PB and J, but I'm sure once you roast your own peppers, you'll find many other ways to use them.

Using a long-handled fork, place the peppers in a paper bag, roll down the top of the bag, and set it aside.

Place the peeled garlic in the bowl of a food processor fitted with a steel blade and pulse it to mince the garlic. Add the rinsed chickpeas, lemon juice, and extra virgin olive oil and process the mixture until smooth.

When the peppers have cooled, remove them from the paper bag. Using clean hands, peel the skin from the peppers and discard the skin.

Cut the peppers open. Remove and discard the seeds and core. Cut the remaining roasted pepper flesh into large chunks.

Add the red-pepper chunks and a small sprinkle of cayenne pepper to the mixture in the food processor.

HOMEMADE PITA CHIPS

4 whole-wheat pita breads

¼ cup extra virgin olive oil

1 teaspoon sea salt

½ cup finely chopped fresh rosemary (optional)

Preheat the oven to 350 degrees on the convection setting. Cut the pitas in half and then cut each half into 3–4 wedges. Brush the wedges on both sides with extra virgin olive oil. Arrange them in a single layer on baking sheets with sides, leaving space between the wedges. Sprinkle them with salt and dust them with finely chopped rosemary.

Bake the pita wedges in the middle of the oven for about 7 minutes. If you are using a conventional (rather than convection) oven setting, turn the wedges over once about halfway through the cooking time.

When the pita chips are crisp and brown, remove them from the oven.

Serves 6

Process all the ingredients until they are well blended. Transfer the Roasted Red-Pepper Hummus to a serving bowl. Cover it and chill it in the refrigerator for about 30 minutes so the flavors will blend.

Serve with Homemade Pita Chips.

Makes about 2 cups, serving 8–10

Root Veggies

Sweet-Potato Puree with Buttermilk and Ginger

3 medium-sized sweet potatoes

1 piece of fresh ginger, about 2 inches long and 1 inch in diameter

¾ cup low-fat or nonfat buttermilk

2 tablespoons real maple syrup

Sea salt

Ground black pepper to taste

Equipment: long-handled fork, microplane grater, cutting board, paring knife, chef's knife, food processor, liquid measuring cup, measuring spoons, medium-sized saucepan

Preheat the oven to 400 degrees.

Wash and dry the sweet potatoes, then pierce them with the tines of a fork.

Place the sweet potatoes on the lower rack in the oven and bake them for approximately 45 minutes or until they are very soft.

Remove the potatoes from the oven and let them cool enough to handle.

Peel the piece of fresh ginger and mince it with a microplane grater. You should have about 1½ tablespoons of grated ginger. Put the ginger into the bowl of a food processor fitted with a steel blade.

When the sweet potatoes have cooled, slice them in half and scoop out the flesh. Discard any brown spots.

Add the sweet potato to the ginger in the bowl of the food processor and puree the mixture, stopping to scrape the sides of the bowl periodically. Add the buttermilk gradually so you can achieve the correct consistency. You want the potatoes to be smooth without lumps but not too liquidy. If the pureed potatoes are too dry, you can add a touch more buttermilk.

Add the maple syrup and process again to blend it in thoroughly.

Turn the potato mixture into a medium-sized saucepan, and add just a light sprinkle of sea salt and about 4–5 turns of freshly ground pepper. Reheat them over medium heat, being careful not to burn the bottom. Serve the sweet potatoes warm. They are good with grilled meats.

Serves 6

Homegrown Carrots with Yogurt Ranch Dressing

1 quart organic nonfat or low-fat yogurt

½ cup low-fat or nonfat buttermilk

3 cloves garlic, finely minced

White parts of 3 scallions (green onions), finely minced

1 small bunch of chives, finely minced (2 tablespoons)

1 small bunch of parsley, finely minced (2 tablespoons)

1 small bunch of dill, finely minced (2 tablespoons)

¼ teaspoon paprika

¼ teaspoon ground (dry) mustard

½ teaspoon sea salt

¼ teaspoon black pepper

1 large bunch of homegrown carrots

Equipment: large spoon, fine-mesh sieve, medium-sized mixing bowl, liquid measuring cup, measuring spoons, garlic mincer, cutting board, chef's knife

Spoon the yogurt into a fine-mesh sieve over a bowl and let the liquid drain into the bowl for a minimum of 20 minutes or overnight in the refrigerator.

Discard the liquid (whey) from the yogurt.

Place the remaining, thick yogurt in a mixing bowl and add ½ cup low-fat or nonfat buttermilk.

Add the minced garlic, scallion, chives, parsley, and dill, as well as the paprika, dry mustard, salt, and pepper to the bowl. Stir well to combine the ingredients and refrigerate the dressing for at least 30 minutes to let the flavors blend.

Serve with julienned carrots.

A PRETTY WAY TO SERVE CRUDITÉS

Use crunchy vegetables such as carrots, red or green bell peppers, and small zucchini.

Julienne your garden vegetables.

Pour about ¼ inch of extra virgin olive oil into the bottoms of small juice glasses or clean votive candleholders and arrange julienned vegetables of different colors in each glass.

Each guest will then have a glass of vegetables with its own "built-in" dip.

Zucchini-Topped Roasted Beets

2 large beets

Marinade:

3 tablespoons extra virgin olive oil

Juice of 1 orange (⅓–½ cup)

1 teaspoon Dijon mustard

1 medium zucchini, washed

Zest of 2 oranges (such as small temple or honey bells)

Orange vinaigrette:

2 tablespoons extra virgin olive oil

Juice of ½ orange

½ teaspoon Dijon mustard

½ cup chopped walnuts

½ cup crumbled goat cheese

Zest the oranges before squeezing them. It's much easier that way.

Equipment: cutting board, vegetable peeler, chef's knife, zester, orange juicer, measuring spoons, dry measuring cups, food processor, pot holders, trivets, baking sheet with sides, medium-sized mixing bowl, small bowl for mixing marinade, small whisk, serving dish

Preheat the oven to 400 degrees in convection mode.

Peel the beets and cut them into thin wedges.

Make a marinade from the extra virgin olive oil, the juice of one orange, and the mustard. Coat the beets with the marinade and place them on a baking sheet with sides. Pour any additional marinade over the beets.

Roast the beets for 30–40 minutes or until they are fork tender and brown on the edges.

Remove the beets from the oven and place them on a serving dish.

Grate the zucchini in a food processor fitted with a grating disk.

Transfer the grated zucchini to a medium-sized mixing bowl, sprinkle on the orange zest, and stir to combine.

Prepare the orange vinaigrette and pour it into the bowl with the zucchini and orange zest, toss until the zucchini is coated, and spoon the mixture on top of the beets.

Top with crumbled goat cheese (or another cheese you prefer) and chopped walnuts.

Serves 6

Roasted Rainbow of Carrots

4 white carrots ('Crème de Lite')
4 red carrots ('Cosmic Purple' and 'Atomic Red')
4 orange carrots ('Danvers')
2 tablespoons extra virgin olive oil
Sea salt (a light sprinkle)

Even if you grow only one color of carrots, you will still enjoy roasting them.

Equipment: cutting board, chef's knife, measuring spoons, large bowl, baking sheet with sides, pot holders, trivets

Preheat the oven to 375 degrees on the convection setting.

Cut off the carrot tops, leaving about an inch of green for appearance.

Wash the carrots well. (Peeling them is optional.)

Homegrown carrots are often small and thin. In this case you can roast them whole. If your carrots are larger, slice them lengthwise in halves or quarters (if a carrot is especially thick). Try to make all the pieces of a similar size so they will cook in the same amount of time.

Place the carrots in the bowl, pour the extra virgin olive oil over them, and rub the oil on the carrots with clean hands until the carrots are coated.

Lay the carrots on a baking sheet with sides. If the carrots are cut, place the cut side down. Drizzle the carrots with any remaining oil.

Roast the carrots for 45 minutes, until carrots are tender and browned. (If you use a conventional oven setting, turn the carrots once, halfway through the cooking time, so they will brown on both sides.)

After you remove the carrots from the oven, you may sprinkle them with a bit of sea salt.

Serves 4

Roasting carrots makes them very flavorful, so you may find folks want more!

Fisherman's Vegetable Stew

- ½ cup extra virgin olive oil
- 2 medium onions, roughly chopped
- 4 stalks of celery, roughly chopped
- 3 cloves garlic, smashed, peeled, and roughly chopped
- 6 plum tomatoes, cut into chunks
- 6 small red potatoes, washed and quartered
- 4 cups DIY Vegetable Stock (recipe on page 136)
- 1 bay leaf
- 3 medium zucchini, washed and cut into bite-sized chunks
- 2½ pounds fresh skinless fish fillets (such as halibut), cut into bite-sized chunks
- Juice of 1 lemon
- ½ cup chopped fresh parsley
- Sea salt and pepper

Equipment: large stockpot, cutting board, chef's knife, fish knife, tomato knife, liquid measuring cup, dry measuring cups, large wooden spoon

Cover the bottom of a large stockpot with the extra virgin olive oil and heat it over medium-high heat.

SEAFOOD SAFETY AND SUSTAINABILITY

Seafood is a great source of healthy fat and protein. My mom used to call it brain food, which research has confirmed. But there are at least four concerns about choosing which foods from the sea are safest.

Some of the larger fish, such as tuna, can be contaminated with mercury. Some farm-raised fish may contain growth hormones. Some wild-caught fish might be overfished, and fishing practices sometimes jeopardize the lives of dolphins and whales that get snared in the large commercial-fishing nets.

I feel that the best way to avoid unhealthy or unsustainable fish is to buy locally caught fish, preferably from local fishermen. We are fortunate to have local farmers markets in our area that include fish-mongers, and there are several seaport towns along the coast where we can buy right from the fishermen.

For guidance in finding sustainable, healthy fish in your area, check the regional Fishery Management Councils information on the National Oceanic and Atmospheric Administration website (http://www.nmfs.noaa.gov/sfa/reg_svcs/councils.htm).

Add the onions and celery, reduce the heat to medium-low, and cook for 5 minutes, stirring with a wooden spoon occasionally.

Add the garlic and cook another 2–3 minutes.

Add the tomatoes, potatoes, DIY Vegetable Stock, and bay leaf.

Turn up the heat, bring the mixture to a boil, and cook it partially covered until the potatoes are fork tender and the stock has been somewhat reduced.

Add the zucchini and cook uncovered for another 5 minutes.

Add the chunks of fish and cook covered at a rolling boil for about 5 minutes, just until the fish is opaque.

Lower the heat to simmer and add the lemon juice and fresh parsley.

Gently stir to combine all ingredients, being careful not to break the fish into little pieces.

Season with sea salt and pepper.

Serve immediately with crusty bread.

Serves 6–8

Carrot and Ginger Soup

- 2 medium-sized yellow onions
- 3 tablespoons extra virgin olive oil
- 3-inch piece of ginger, peeled
- 12 medium carrots
- 4 cups DIY Vegetable Stock (recipe on page 136)
- Zest of 2 washed oranges
- Juice of 2 oranges
- Sea salt and freshly ground black pepper

Equipment: large stockpot, cutting board, chef's knife, vegetable peeler, wooden spoon, slotted spoon, colander, large bowl, food processor, ladle, measuring spoons, liquid measuring cup, orange juicer, microplane grater, zester, food processor, serving bowls

Peel and finely chop the yellow onions.

Heat the extra virgin olive oil in the large stockpot over medium heat and add the onions.

Cook the onions slowly until they are tender and translucent, about 15 minutes. While the onions are cooking, grate the ginger with a microplane grater and stir the minced ginger into the onions.

Stir the mixture occasionally with a wooden spoon.

Peel the carrots and cut them into 1½-inch pieces.

Add the DIY Vegetable Stock and carrots to the pot, turn up the heat, bring the soup to a boil, and then lower heat so the soup is simmering.

Simmer the soup until the carrots are very soft, about 30 minutes.

Turn off the heat, and pour the soup into a colander set on a large bowl in the sink.

Transfer the solids to the bowl of a food processor fitted with a metal blade. Using a ladle, add one cup of the soup liquid to the food processor. Process the contents until they are smooth,

Zest the oranges, being careful to avoid the white pith, which is bitter. Squeeze the oranges and remove any seeds from the juice.

Pour the puree into the stockpot, add the orange juice, and 2–3 cups of the remaining soup liquid, until you have the desired texture.

Reheat the soup, taste it, and season it lightly with sea salt and freshly ground black pepper.

When serving the soup, top each bowl with grated orange zest.

Serves 4–6

Roasted Winter-Vegetable Soup

- 2 leeks
- 6 stalks of celery
- 4 carrots, peeled
- 4 small potatoes, peeled
- 4 parsnips, peeled
- 4 beets, peeled
- ⅓ cup extra virgin olive oil
- 3 cups DIY Vegetable Stock (recipe on page 136)
- 1 teaspoon sea salt
- Freshly ground black pepper to taste
- Fresh greens (optional)
- Chopped sage or thyme for garnish

Equipment: clean kitchen towel, liquid measuring cup, measuring spoons, large baking sheet with sides, aluminum foil, pot holders, food processor, large saucepan

Preheat the oven to 375 degrees on the convection setting.

Leeks tend to harbor a fair amount of soil within them. To clean the leeks, first cut off the dark green parts and put them in your kitchen compost bucket. Take the remaining leeks and, starting in the white part, slice them vertically in three or four places all the way up to the light green part.

Submerge the leeks in warm water for 5 minutes, shake them around in the water, and then rinse them thoroughly with cool water. Dry the leeks on a clean kitchen towel.

Chop all the vegetables into large chunks and spread them out on a baking sheet with sides.

Pour the extra virgin olive oil over the vegetables and, with clean hands, rub the veggies with the oil to coat them on all sides.

Roast the vegetables covered with aluminum foil for 30 minutes and then uncover them and roast for another 30 minutes. The vegetables should be very soft.

Puree the vegetables in a food processor fitted with a steel blade.

Transfer the puree to a large saucepan. Add the DIY Vegetable Stock, sea salt, and black pepper and reheat the soup on the stove top over medium-high heat.

If fresh spinach, kale, turnip greens, or mustard greens are available, you may chop some and add them to the soup before heating it. Cook the soup just until the greens are wilted. If not, simply heat the soup as is until it boils.

Add chopped sage or thyme for garnish.

Serves 6 as dinner portions

Parsleyed Meatballs in Cinnamony Tomato Sauce

Parsleyed Meatballs:

4–5 thin slices of stale, whole-wheat bread

½ cup dry red wine

1½ pounds of lean chopped beef, such as sirloin

1 egg, slightly beaten

1 clove garlic, peeled and minced

1 teaspoon ground cumin

½ cup finely chopped parsley

Salt and pepper

3 tablespoons extra virgin olive oil

Cinnamony Tomato Sauce:

4 cups finely chopped tomatoes (about 7 medium tomatoes)

2 tablespoons tomato paste

½ cup dry red wine

1 scant teaspoon of sugar

1 teaspoon cinnamon

1 bay leaf

1 teaspoon sea salt

A few grinds of black pepper

Equipment: large mixing bowl, large sauté pan, large spoon, liquid measuring cup, dry measuring cup, measuring spoons, cutting board, chef's knife, small bowl, fork or small whisk, garlic press, plate covered with a paper towel

Cut the crusts from the stale bread and discard them. Tear the bread into pieces, place them into a large mixing bowl, and pour the red wine over them.

Add the remaining ingredients for the meatballs (except the extra virgin olive oil) and stir them with a large spoon to combine. The mixture will be quite wet.

Using clean hands, shape the meat mixture into egg-sized oval meatballs.

Heat the extra virgin olive oil in a large sauté pan over medium-high heat.

Carefully place several of the meatballs in the hot oil and brown them on all sides. Turn the meatballs as little as possible so as not to break them.

When the meatballs are browned, move them to a plate covered with a paper towel to absorb excess oil. Continue browning meatballs until they are all done.

Using the same pan in which you cooked the meatballs, stir together all the ingredients for Cinnamony Tomato Sauce with a wooden spoon. Cook the sauce for about 10 minutes over medium heat, keeping the sauce at a simmer. Remove the bay leaf.

Add the meatballs to the sauce and cook for another 10 minutes. Remove the pan from the heat.

Serve immediately or reheat before serving.

Serves 6–8

If your bread is not stale, leave it uncovered in the air for a bit to dry it.

The Best Basil Pesto

¼ cup pine nuts
3 medium cloves garlic
2 full cups fresh basil leaves
¼ cup fresh parsley leaves
7 tablespoons extra virgin olive oil
½ teaspoon sea salt
¼ cup grated Parmesan, Romano, Asiago, or pecorino cheese

Equipment: dry measuring cup, measuring spoons, small sauté pan, wooden spoon, 2 small bowls, large cutting board, chef's knife, rolling pin, food processor, rubber spatula, small covered storage bowl

Toast the pine nuts in a small sauté pan over medium heat. Shake the pan occasionally, or stir the nuts with a wooden spoon until they are golden brown on all sides, about 4 minutes. Pour the nuts into a small bowl.

Add the cloves of garlic (in their skins) to the same pan and toast them in the same way for about 5 minutes. Remove the garlic to a cutting board, let it cool, and then smash the cloves with your chef's knife, remove the skin, and chop the garlic.

Set the chopped garlic aside in a small bowl.

Pile the basil and parsley leaves on a large cutting board, roughly chop them, and roll over them several times with a rolling pin. This process bruises the leaves and allows the flavor to be released.

Place the pine nuts, garlic, basil and parsley leaves, extra virgin olive oil, and sea salt in a food processor fitted with a steel blade and process the mixture until it is smooth and well blended. You may have to stop the food processor once or twice to scrape down the sides of the bowl with a rubber spatula.

Transfer the mixture to a small bowl. Stir in the grated cheese.

You can store the pesto in the refrigerator for 3 days in an airtight container.

To enjoy the Best Basil Pesto over pasta, prepare the pasta according to the package directions. When it is ready, reserve ⅓ cup of the cooking water before you drain the pasta.

Mix the reserved pasta water with the pesto to thin it, stirring well. Toss the hot pasta with the pesto.

Serve immediately.

Serves 4

I have a friend who freezes pesto in an ice-cube tray and pops out a few cubes at a time to add to her tomato sauce for a nice herbal brightness, especially in the dead of winter.

BASIL

With any luck by the end of the summer, your garden will be overflowing with fragrant basil plants just days away from flowering—*PESTO TIME!*

But what if you can't make time for pesto time? Lidia Bastianich of PBS cooking-show fame says you can freeze basil leaves in zip-lock bags of water, and the leaves won't turn black. Definitely worth a try.

Broiled Shrimp with Garlic and Oregano

1 pound large shrimp (approximately 33)
½ cup extra virgin olive oil
6 cloves garlic, peeled
3 teaspoons dried oregano
Juice of 1 lemon
½ teaspoon sea salt
½ cup finely chopped parsley for garnish
Lemon wedges for garnish

If you are using wooden skewers, soak them briefly in water first so they won't burn.

Equipment: liquid measuring cup, dry measuring cup, measuring spoons, garlic press, small saucepan, large mixing bowl, wooden spoon, skewers, broiler pan, basting brush, pot holders

Shell and devein the shrimp (see directions on page 98), but leave the tails in place.

Heat 2 tablespoons of the extra virgin olive oil in a small saucepan over medium heat.

Mince the garlic using a garlic press. Warm the minced garlic and the dried oregano in the oil, stirring it with a wooden spoon for 2 minutes. Do not brown it.

Remove the pan from the heat and pour the contents into a large mixing bowl. Stir in the remaining extra virgin olive oil, the lemon juice, and the salt to create a marinade.

Add the cleaned shrimp to the bowl and toss the shrimp until the marinade covers it. Let the shrimp sit in the marinade for at least 30 minutes.

When you are ready to cook the shrimp preheat the broiler.

Put 3–4 shrimp onto each skewer, place them on the broiler pan, and brush the shrimp with the remaining marinade.

Broil the shrimp for about 2 minutes per side, until they are pink and firm.

Using potholders, remove the pan from the broiler, then transfer the skewers of grilled shrimp onto a platter and sprinkle finely chopped parsley over them. Serve with lemon wedges.

Serves 6

Tabbouleh with Herbs, Dried Fruit, and Nuts

Equipment: medium-sized bowl, wooden spoon, plate, small bowl, colander, dry measuring cups, liquid measuring cup, measuring spoons, cutting board, chef's knife, garlic press, lemon juicer, large bowl

- 1 cup fine bulgur
- Juice of 2 lemons
- 1 cup boiling water
- 1 small red onion, finely chopped
- 3 cloves garlic, minced
- 1 cup minced fresh parsley leaves
- ¼ cup minced mint leaves (no stems)
- ½ cup finely chopped dried apricots
- ½ cup shelled pistachio nuts
- ½ cup extra virgin olive oil
- Sea salt and black pepper to taste

Put the bulgur in a medium-sized bowl and pour the juice of 1 lemon and 1 cup of boiling water over it. Stir to combine, cover the bowl with a plate, and set it aside.

Place the finely chopped red onion, minced garlic, minced parsley, minced mint leaves (no stems), chopped dried apricots, and pistachio nuts in a large bowl.

After about 30 minutes, the bulgur should look fluffy and be tender. Depending on the cut of bulgur you have used, the water may be fully absorbed or there may be some remaining. If there is still some water in the bowl, drain the bulgur in a fine mesh sieve and discard the water.

Add the bulgur to the large bowl and stir in the remaining lemon juice and the extra virgin olive oil until all ingredients are combined.

Taste the tabbouleh and add a little sea salt and black pepper to taste.

Chill the tabbouleh for about 1–2 hours before serving it to allow all the flavors to blend. Tabbouleh is even better on the second day, and tabbouleh and hummus make a great combination!

Serves 8

Bulgur comes in fine, medium, coarse, and very coarse grades. Fine is the bulgur of choice for tabbouleh.

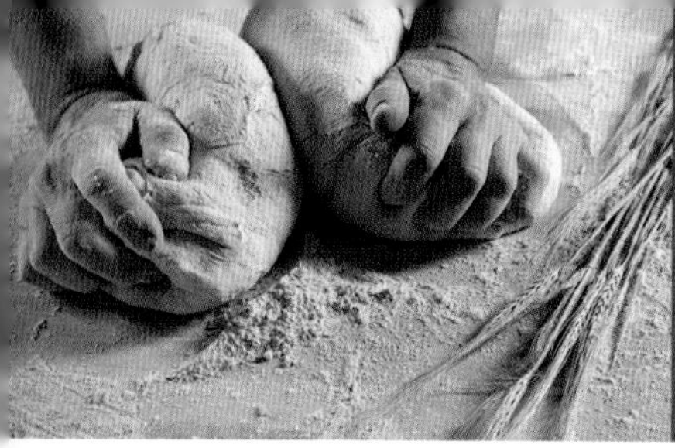

Basics

Whole-Wheat Pizza Crust

- 1 package active dry yeast
- ¼ cup warm water
- 1 teaspoon sugar
- 1¼ cups whole-wheat flour
- 2 cups unbleached all-purpose flour
- 3 tablespoons extra virgin olive oil, plus a bit more for oiling the bowl
- 1 tablespoon honey
- ½ teaspoon sea salt
- 1 cup warm water
- 1 teaspoon corn meal

Equipment: pizza stone, liquid measuring cup, dry measuring cups, measuring spoons, small whisk, food processor (optional), large bowl, clean kitchen towel or plastic wrap, large wooden cutting board, pot holders, large trivet, fork, large spoon, metal spatula, pizza cutter

Dissolve the yeast in a liquid measuring cup with ¼ cup lukewarm water and 1 teaspoon sugar. Stir the mixture with a small whisk. The yeast should double in size in 10 minutes, signaling that it is active.

In the bowl of a food processor fitted with a steel blade, combine the yeast and water mixture, the whole-wheat flour, unbleached all-purpose flour, extra virgin olive oil, honey, salt, and 1 cup of warm water. Pulse about eight times, until all ingredients are combined and form a large lump of dough.

Turn the dough onto a floured cutting board and knead it with floured hands for only about 1 minute. Press and push it into the board, gently but firmly.

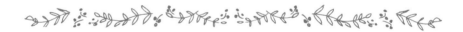

ACTIVE DRY YEAST

Yeast is a microorganism (a tiny living plant) that exists in soil, on vegetation, and in the air. Yeast aids in fermentation.

Active dry yeast (*Saccharomyces cerevisiae*) is used to make bread and pizza doughs rise because it converts sugar into carbon dioxide (CO_2). Without yeast, breads and pizza crusts would be heavy and dense.

Move it around so each part of the dough is gently kneaded. Shape the dough into two balls.

Coat the sides and bottom of a large bowl with extra virgin olive oil. To make one pizza, add one ball of dough and cover the bowl with a clean kitchen towel or plastic wrap. The second dough ball can be wrapped in plastic wrap and kept in the refrigerator for 3–4 days or frozen for future use.

Set the bowl in a warm place and allow the dough to rise for 45 minutes or until it has doubled in size. I usually put mine inside the oven (with the heat turned off). If your kitchen is really cold—think winter in Vermont or highly air-conditioned summer in South Carolina—you can place the bowl in a *prewarmed* oven to rise. Preheat the oven to 150 degrees and then shut it off before you place the bowl of dough in the oven.

When the dough has risen, remove it from the oven. Preheat the oven to 500 degrees with the pizza stone inside so it preheats too.

Place the dough ball on a floured cutting board. Punch it down. You may see bulges of dough pop as the air is pushed out of it.

EXTRA-SPECIAL HERBED PIZZA CRUST

To add pizzazz to your pizza crust, try adding chopped fresh herbs to your basic pizza dough. When you are combining the ingredients, add ¼ cup of any one of the following, finely chopped:

- rosemary
- oregano leaves
- sage or thyme
- basil leaves
- scallions, or
- 3–4 cloves of garlic, minced

Press the ball into a flat circle. Starting in the middle of the circle, use your fingertips to press the dough, pushing it outward in a circular pattern to broaden the circle.

Turn over the circle of dough, lightly flour it, and using a rolling pin, roll the dough away from you, turning the whole cutting board one quarter of a circle after each roll so the rolling pin will stretch all the dough into a larger circle. Continue rolling and stretching the dough until it is about ⅛ inch thick.

Place a large trivet on your workspace. Very carefully, with good, dry pot holders, remove the hot pizza stone from the oven and place it on the trivet.

Sprinkle the pizza stone with corn meal.

Lift up your pizza dough with both hands and place it on the pizza stone—being careful not to touch the stone.

Prick the crust here and there with the tines of a fork.

Prebake the pizza crust for 6–7 minutes or until the bottom is brown when you lift it with a metal spatula to check it.

Using your pot holders, carefully remove the pizza stone from the oven and place it on the trivet.

Spoon whatever sauce you are using onto the pizza crust, and spread it around with the back of a large spoon to cover the crust, leaving about a one-inch plain edge.

Add whatever solid toppings you are using.

Using your pot holders, return the pizza stone with the fully dressed pizza to the hot oven and bake it for approximately 8–10 minutes or until the toppings are cooked as desired, the cheese has melted, and the sauce is bubbling hot.

Using your pot holders, remove the pizza stone from the oven and slide your pizza creation onto a clean wooden cutting board.

Let the pizza stand for a few minutes and then slice it into wedges with a pizza cutter.

Serves 4–6

DIY Vegetable Stock

1 whole bulb garlic
2 large onions, peeled
4 medium carrots, peeled
1 bunch green carrot tops, washed
¼ head cabbage with core, washed
1 large radish, washed and cut in half
4 stalks celery, washed
10 peppercorns
2 bay leaves
½ gallon water

Feel free to experiment by adding other garden vegetables and herbs, but please know that, though dark green potato leaves might look like a good choice, they are in fact poisonous!

Equipment: liquid measuring cup, large stockpot, cutting board, chef's knife, fine mesh sieve, large bowl

Separate the garlic cloves and smash them with the handle of a heavy chef's knife to remove the skins.

Roughly chop all the vegetables. Place all ingredients in a large stockpot and add about ½ gallon water.

Cover the pot and bring the water to a boil over high heat. Turn down the heat, move the pot lid to allow some steam to escape, and simmer for an hour.

Strain the stock through a fine mesh sieve into a large bowl. Set aside the solids to snack on or discard.

This is your basic vegetable stock. Notice it has no sea salt yet. When you use it in recipes, you can taste it after adding the other ingredients and add a bit of sea salt if needed at that time.

Store the stock in covered jars in your refrigerator. It will last about 5 days.

All-Clad

Fruits

Real Fruit Sodas

½ glass juice of your choice (such as cherry, pomegranate, or orange)

½ glass sodium-free seltzer

A squeeze of lime juice (wash the lime first) or a bit of fresh mint (wash the mint)

Fruit sodas are fun to make, especially using fresh-squeezed juice. They are refreshing and not too sweet.

Equipment: cutting board, paring knife, iced-tea spoon

Combine the juice and seltzer over ice, stir with an iced-tea spoon, and add a squeeze of fresh lime juice and/or a sprig of fresh mint.

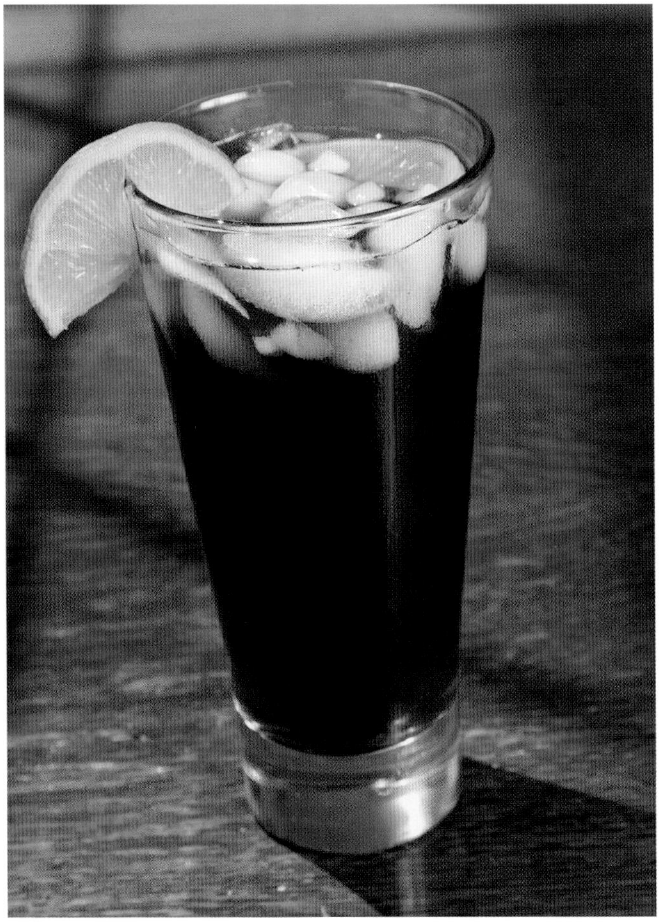

Nut-Crusted Creamy Almond and Fruit Tart

Equipment: dry measuring cups, measuring spoons, cutting board, paring knife, medium-sized bowl, electric mixer (with flat-beater and wire-whip attachments and mixing bowl), 4 individual tart pans (fluted, with removable bottoms) or a 9-inch tart pan (fluted, with removable bottom), pastry brush, measuring cups, food processor, wire cooling rack

Fruit Topping:

2 cups ripe strawberries

1 teaspoon sugar

Crust:

½ cup macadamia nuts

¼ cup walnuts

½ cup almonds

¼ cup shelled pistachios

½ cup cashews

3 tablespoons unsalted butter (at room temperature)

¼ cup white whole-wheat flour

3 tablespoons white sugar

3 tablespoons brown sugar

3 egg whites

Canola oil and flour to prepare pans

Filling:

½ cup almond paste

2 teaspoons white sugar

1½ tablespoons milk (nonfat is fine)

1 8-ounce container mascarpone cheese (at room temperature)

Preheat the oven to 275 degrees.

Rinse the strawberries and cut off the green tops. (Put the tops in your kitchen compost bucket.)

Thinly slice the strawberries, place them in a bowl, and sprinkle them with 1 teaspoon of sugar. Set the berries aside.

Place all the nuts in the bowl of a food processor fitted with a steel blade. Process the nuts until they are finely chopped but not ground into flour. (Three medium pulses should do it.)

Cut the butter into chunks and put it in a mixing bowl.

Add the nuts, flour, and sugars. Using the flat-beater attachment for the mixer, mix the crust ingredients until they are well combined.

With the mixer running, add the egg whites one at a time and mix until they are well incorporated into the dough, which should look blended and glossy.

Prepare the tart pans by coating them with canola oil and flour. First use a brush or paper towel to cover the inside surfaces of each pan with the oil. Then sprinkle the inside with a little flour and shake it to coat it entirely with the flour. Finally turn the pan upside down over the sink (holding onto the pan bottom so it doesn't fall out), and shake out any excess flour.

You can buy raw nuts and "roast" them yourself. Place them in an ungreased sauté pan over moderate heat. Stir them with a wooden spoon and cook just until they begin to brown.

If using individual tart pans, divide the nut "dough" into four equal parts. Using clean hands, press it into the tart pans, covering the bottoms and sides.

Place the tart pans on a cookie sheet and put the cookie sheet in the center of the oven.

Bake the tart crusts for about 20 minutes, until they are set and beginning to brown. They will continue to brown as they cool.

When the crusts are ready, remove them from the oven and set them aside on a wire cooling rack.

Wash the food processor and reassemble it.

Cut the almond paste into chunks and place it in the food processor. Add 2 teaspoons white sugar and the 1½ tablespoons milk. Process this mixture until the almond paste thins and smoothes out and all the ingredients are well combined.

Fit the electric mixer with a wire whip and transfer the almond-paste mixture to the clean mixing bowl. Add the mascarpone cheese and beat the mixture well until all the ingredients are combined and smooth.

Fill the tarts with the almond-paste and mascarpone mixture.

Top the tarts with the sliced strawberries.

Serve immediately or refrigerate.

Serves 4 individual tarts or 6 in larger tart pan.

Spiced Poached Pears with Creamy Yogurt and Blueberry Compote

- 1 quart plain organic low-fat or nonfat yogurt
- 4 firm-ripe pears (not rock hard or mushy soft)
- 4 cups apple cider
- ½ teaspoon ground cardamom
- ½ teaspoon ground cinnamon
- ¼ teaspoon ground cloves
- ¼ teaspoon ground ginger
- 4 small basil leaves for garnish (optional)

Equipment: fine-mesh sieve, small bowl, 4–8 small serving bowls, paring knife, cutting board, teaspoon, fork, large pot, liquid measuring cup, measuring spoons, slotted spoon, large bowl, wooden spoon

Drain the yogurt by spooning it into a fine-mesh sieve sitting over a small bowl. Set the yogurt aside.

Peel the pears and slice them in half lengthwise. Using a teaspoon, remove the cores. Trim off the stems with a paring knife.

In a large pot bring the cider and spices to a boil and carefully drop the pear halves into the liquid. Reduce the heat to a simmer and poach the pears uncovered until a fork easily pierces a pear (about 25 minutes).

Remove the pear halves with a slotted spoon, place them in a bowl, and let them cool to room temperature.

Transfer the thickened yogurt to a bowl and discard the liquid (whey).

Before serving, top each poached pear half with a heaping tablespoon of strained plain yogurt. Then top the yogurt with Blueberry Compote and garnish with tiny basil leaves.

Serves 4–8

Save the cider you poached the pears in, strain it through a fine-mesh sieve, and warm it over medium heat to enjoy spiced cider on a cold day.

Blueberry Compote

Equipment: dry measuring cups, measuring spoons, colander, medium-sized saucepan, lemon zester, wooden spoon

4 cups whole blueberries
Zest of one lemon
Juice of one lemon
1 teaspoon ground cinnamon
Juice of one orange
⅓ cup brown sugar

Wash the blueberries and drain them in a colander set in the sink.

Rinse and zest the lemon.

In a medium saucepan combine 3 cups of the blueberries with the lemon juice, cinnamon, orange juice, and the zest of one lemon.

Cook the mixture over moderate heat, stirring occasionally with a wooden spoon until it begins to boil. Lower the heat to a simmer and cook for about 5 minutes—now stirring all the while with a wooden spoon—until the mixture reduces and begins to thicken. The berries will begin to burst.

Add the brown sugar and cook while stirring for another 5 minutes. The compote will be a beautiful purple color and should be thick enough to coat the back of a spoon.

Remove the pan from heat and stir in the remaining blueberries.

Let the compote cool at room temperature or place it in the refrigerator until it is no longer warm.

Spoon the compote over the tops of the Spiced Poached Pears with Creamy Yogurt.

Makes about 3 cups

This blueberry compote is also delicious instead of strawberries on Nut-Crusted Creamy Almond Fruit Tart (page 139) or with Blanched Peaches (page 144).

Blanched Peaches

6 ripe peaches

Water

Equipment: large pot, colander, large bowl, paring knife, long rectangular airtight container

Bring a large pot of water to a boil on the stovetop and carefully drop the peaches into it. Let the peaches cook for 2 minutes, then drain them in a colander in the sink.

Immediately "shock" the peaches by placing them into an ice-water bath in a large bowl.

When the peaches are cool enough to handle, peel them and slice each one in half along its natural seam.

Remove the pits and store the blanched peach halves in an airtight container in the refrigerator.

Serve the peach halves for breakfast filled with plain strained yogurt, chopped walnuts, and a drizzle of honey, or fill the peaches with Blueberry Compote (page 143) and serve them as a dessert.

Serves 12

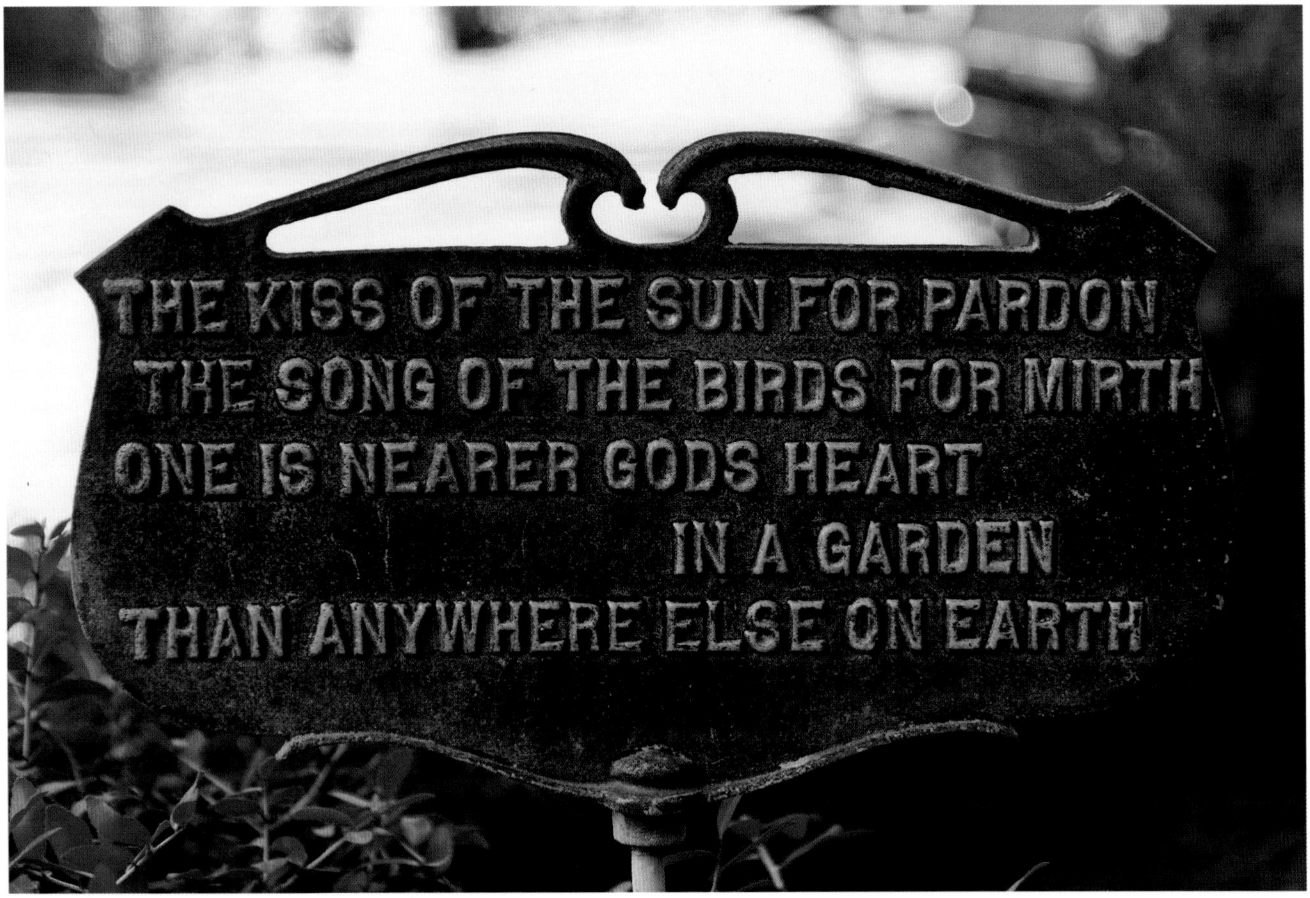
THE KISS OF THE SUN FOR PARDON
THE SONG OF THE BIRDS FOR MIRTH
ONE IS NEARER GODS HEART
IN A GARDEN
THAN ANYWHERE ELSE ON EARTH

References

NUTRITION

Campbell, T. Colin, with Thomas M. Campbell II. *The China Study: The Most Comprehensive Study of Nutrition Ever Conducted and the Startling Implications for Diet, Weight Loss, and Long-Term Health.* Dallas: Benbella Books, 2005.

Carpenter, Ruth Ann, and Carrie E. Finley. *Healthy Eating Every Day.* Champaign, Ill.: Human Kinetics, 2005.

Centers for Disease Control and Prevention website. Online at http://www.cdc.gov/ (accessed October 15, 2012).

Dole Nutrition Institute. *The Dole Nutrition Handbook: What You Need to Eat and How to Live for a Longer, Healthier Life.* Emmaus, Pa.: Rodale, 2010.

Editors of *Cook's Illustrated. The New Best Recipe.* Brookline, Mass.: America's Test Kitchen, 2004.

Harvard University School of Public Health, Department of Nutrition. *The Nutrition Source: Knowledge for Healthy Eating.* Online at http://www.hsph.harvard.edu/nutritionsource/ (accessed October 15, 2012).

Hyman, Mark, and Mark Liponis. *Ultraprevention: The Six-Week Plan That Will Make You Healthy for Life.* New York: Scribner, 2003.

National Institutes of Health, Office of Dietary Supplements. *Dietary Supplement Fact Sheets.* Online at http://ods.od.nih.gov/ (accessed October 15, 2012).

Shryer, Donna, with Stephen Dawson. *Body Fuel: A Guide to Good Nutrition.* Tarrytown, N.Y.: Marshall Cavendish, 2010.

Virtual Chembook. Online at http://www.elmhurst.edu/~chm/vchembook/index.html (accessed June 9, 2012).

GARDENING

Auch, Alison J. *Garden Tools.* Minneapolis: Compass Point Books, 2003.

Bird, Richard. *Planning a Kitchen Garden: A Practical Design Manual for Growing Fruits, Herbs, and Vegetables.* London: Southwater, 2009.

Chase, Nan K. *Eat Your Yard! Edible Trees, Shrubs, Vines, Herbs, and Flowers for Your Landscape.* Layton, Utah: Gibbs Smith, 2010.

Clemson Cooperative Extension. *Home & Garden Information Center.* Online at http://www.clemson.edu/extension/hgic/ (accessed October 15, 2012).

Henderson, Kathy. *And the Good Brown Earth.* Cambridge, Mass.: Candlewick Press, 2004.

"Kid's Garden Site." Online at http://homeandgardensite.com/ChildrensSite/index.htm (accessed October 15, 2012).

Snyder, Inez. *Gardening Tools.* New York: Children's Press, 2002.

Teegan, Marta. *Homegrown: A Growing Guide for Creating a Cook's Garden.* Emmaus, Pa.: Rodale, 2010.

University of California Agriculture and Natural Resources. *Soil Solarization for Gardens & Landscapes.* Pest Notes Publication 74145 (October 2008). Online at http://www.ipm.ucdavis.edu/PMG/PESTNOTES/pn74145.html (accessed June 26, 2012).

University of Illinois Extension. *My First Garden: A Guide to the World of Fun & Clever Gardening.* Online at http://urbanext.illinois.edu/firstgarden/ (accessed October 15, 2012).

Vanderlinden, Colleen. "Best Vegetables to Grow in the Shade." *Mother Earth News,* February–March 2011. Online at http://www.motherearthnews.com/organic-gardening/vegetables-to-grow-in-shade-zmoz11zsto.aspx (accessed June 10, 2012).

Whitehouse, Patty. *Plant and Prune.* Vero Beach, Fla.: Rourke, 2007.

Index

Patricia Moore-Pastides is the First Lady of the University of South Carolina, where she teaches healthy Mediterranean cooking classes for USC students. In addition Moore-Pastides, who earned a master's in public health from Yale University, teaches adults and children through Columbia's Cooking!, a community program offered by the University's Cancer Prevention and Control Program. As part of being an active participant in Healthy Carolina's farmers' market, she cultivates an organic vegetable garden at the President's House. Moore-Pastides also works to support sustainability initiatives on campus and lectures on wellness, specifically the health benefits of the traditional Mediterranean diet and lifestyle. She is the author of *Greek Revival: Cooking for Life*.